Workplace Intelligei

Workplace Intelligence provides a range of insights into the unconscious processes at play in the workplace and an introduction to a balanced approach to organizations.

The book explores key concepts, showing how our emotions and early experiences inform the roles we play at work, as well as how we react to other people. It encourages close observation and reflection and utilization of this knowledge for managing ourselves and others fruitfully. It also provides managers with the methods to intervene and tackle these issues, elaborating on topics from leadership and group dynamics to meetings and work–life balance.

The book will be a fascinating read for those in leadership roles, organizational consultants, executive coaches, students of occupational psychology, as well as anyone interested in understanding workplace dynamics in general.

Anton Obholzer is a psychiatrist and psychoanalyst who, through his role as Chief Executive of the Tavistock & Portman NHS Trust, became interested in applying his professional knowledge to workplaces. He has been influential in developing alternative management courses and has taught throughout Europe on business programmes as well as other extensive coaching and consulting.

Workplace Intelligence

Unconscious Forces and How to Manage Them

Anton Obholzer

Routledge
Taylor & Francis Group
LONDON AND NEW YORK

First published 2021
by Routledge
2 Park Square, Milton Park, Abingdon, Oxon OX14 4RN

and by Routledge
52 Vanderbilt Avenue, New York, NY 10017

Routledge is an imprint of the Taylor & Francis Group, an informa business

© 2021 Anton Obholzer

British Library Cataloguing-in-Publication Data
A catalogue record for this book is available from the British Library

Library of Congress Cataloging-in-Publication Data
Names: Obholzer, Anton, 1938- author.
Title: Workplace intelligence : unconscious forces and how to
manage them / Anton Obholzer.
Description: Abingdon, Oxon; New York, NY: Routledge, 2021.
Identifiers: LCCN 2020031485 (print) | LCCN 2020031486
(ebook) | ISBN 9780367225582 (hardback) | ISBN
9780367225599 (paperback) | ISBN 9780429275630 (ebook)
Subjects: LCSH: Psychology, Industrial. | Management—
Psychological aspects. | Work—Psychological aspects. |
Organizational behavior. | Organizational sociology.
Classification: LCC HF5548.8 .O1876 2021 (print) |
LCC HF5548.8 (ebook) | DDC 158.7—dc23
LC record available at https://lccn.loc.gov/2020031485
LC ebook record available at https://lccn.loc.gov/2020031486

ISBN: 9780367225582 (hbk)
ISBN: 9780367225599 (pbk)
ISBN: 9780429275630 (ebk)

Typeset in Bembo
by codeMantra

For Annabel

'By three methods we may learn wisdom; first, by reflection, which is the noblest; second, by imitation, which is easiest; and third by experience, which is the bitterest'.

Confucius

'At an early stage I had accepted the "bon mot" which lays down that there are three impossible professions: educating; healing; and governing'.

Sigmund Freud

Contents

Foreword

Manfred F. R. Kets de Vries

It is now many years ago when having to be in London for a consulting assignment I decided to combine it with a meeting of the editorial board of the journal *Human Relations* of which I was one of the members. I still remember vividly – having just taken a seat at the table in the meeting room – the entry of an avuncular gentleman, who plopped down in the empty chair beside me. This person was Anton Obholzer. Later, I inferred that his positioning beside me didn't happen by mere chance. I think that he deliberately wanted to sit there, to get a sense of me. I guess, the initial assessment must have been somewhat positive as we continued our relationship over the years. In particular, during the time that I was the Director of INSEAD's Global Leadership Centre, and one of the core faculty members of the Executive Master's in Coaching and Consulting for Change, I came to appreciate Anton's way of looking at the world. In that period, he played an invaluable role in assisting me in creating a well-functioning coaching community. Not only was he very much appreciated and admired by all the executives who were exposed to his wisdom and wit when coaching them, he played a very important role within the coaching group. His creative insights and his subversive sense of humour provided the glue for better working relationships among our team of coaches. Furthermore, in his informal 'supervisory' role, Anton was very adept in dealing with the emerging anxieties that are part of any coaching intervention. He was a great 'container'.

Over time, I discovered that we are kindred souls. We are both 'morosophs', meaning wise fools in the way we deal with the irrationality (or better, the alternative forms of rationality) found in organizational life. In that respect we are soul mates, playing the constructive delinquency game with mischief and pleasure, as a way of creating better places to work – a *Weltanschauung* that's still very dear to us both.

Perhaps Anton's personal history offers some explanations about his peculiar way of looking at the world. The diverse landscape and impressions he had while growing up in South Africa must have been bewildering. I am referring to the fact that his parents were Austrian immigrants to that country. Growing up in a racially divided country in a German-speaking home must have been a fertile ground for a host of vivid and contradictory impressions. Observing the great injustice of the situation, and trying to rise above it, were qualities that would stand him in good stead during his later years in his roles as psychiatrist/psychoanalyst, and Chief Executive of the Tavistock & Portman Clinics.

The first thing that came to mind, after reading Anton's new book *Workplace Intelligence*, was 'bricoleur'. Anton has an unusual ability to mix various ways of thinking in order to address a specific issue or problem. Generally speaking, bricolage is the skill of using whatever is at hand and recombining these parts to create something new. And as a bricoleur, Anton looks at highly complex issues in a very disarming, disorganized, and seemingly non-rational fashion, to subsequently come up with very creative but also highly pragmatic resolutions. As a bricoleur, he is a master of the *Matryoshka*, the Russian nesting doll way of investigation, deciphering the intrapsychic, interpersonal, team, and organizational layers that simultaneously operate in organizational life. It makes him an astute observer, carefully and intuitively interpreting how unconscious processes manifest themselves in individuals and in organizations. Furthermore, due to his deep understanding of the vicissitudes of human behaviour, he is also a very good storyteller, bringing a refreshing look when describing the strengths and foibles of everyday organizational life.

Through clinical vignettes, Anton takes his readers on a deep dive into the day-to-day occurrences of the unconscious dynamics in the workplace, carefully describing what's happening under the surface. His observations are not only sophisticated but also sharp-witted and provocatively amusing. As he says himself:

> a degree of awareness of the existence and dynamic of such processes can make the difference between relative success and relative failure … Placing observation and thoughtfulness at the

centre of the leadership approach has certain key implications for both the leader and the organization.

Anton keeps on reminding us that apart from 'the conscious concrete roles that people perform, there are also other processes at work that, if unchecked, can interfere with the decision-making processes and the task'. And according to him, each organizational participant needs to create a space for observation, reflection, and action that will be essential for future development.

Through the use of vivid colloquial metaphors such as 'pit canary', or 'letting sleeping dogs lie', Anton makes complex unconscious phenomena accessible. Furthermore, his discussion of important psychological concepts such as containment, transference, defensive reactions, splitting, envy, primary task, primary risk, not being on-task, family dynamics, pseudo-mutuality, the role of emotions, early childhood experiences and their role in leadership development, rivalry, mid-life issues, stress reactions in organizational life, meeting management, life transitions, manic defences, retirement, and leader–follower interactions, are second to none in its hard-nosed understanding of organizational life. Also, Anton makes it clear that leaving our private/personal life outside the setting of work would be a major mistake. For reasons of maintaining mental health, he is a strong advocate of an appropriate work–life balance. Only by working in a 'balanced' way can people who work in organizations make positive contributions to home life and organizational life.

Beyond just observations and diagnosis, Anton also suggests practical ways of tackling below the surface issues. He describes different kinds of interventions such as using imagery, and associations to the imagery, that can provide executives with insight about their major preoccupations whether these occur consciously or unconsciously. In the context of facilitating change, he also cautions the reader against emerging resistances: 'Both individuals and organizations generally pay enthusiastic lip service to the idea of growth and development, whereas in reality these processes are experienced as unsettling, disturbing, and uncomfortable, and are thus often resisted with all our unconscious might'. Furthermore, he astutely suggests that we read 'the unconscious subtitles as they appear, but when to feed them back, if at all, is a matter of judgment involving both timing and language'.

In terms of organizational consulting, Anton sees this role as a 'visiting anthropologist' whose responsibility is 'to observe and comment on the behaviour of staff and the contents of their discussion'. The consultant should also be able to engage in 'Licensed Stupidity', which involves the courage to point out the difference between what people say they do, and what they actually do. And in that respect, he is in good company. Wasn't it the management guru, Peter Drucker, who used to say: 'my greatest strength as a consultant is to be ignorant and ask a few questions'. Furthermore Anton points out that the stated problem often turns out not to be the real problem. This leads him to the idea of the consultant-in-the-mind of the client – the question of what the consultant symbolizes to the client. He cautions that consultants should not become part of a *folie-a-deux* with the client, engaging in a self-fulfilling prophecy of ritualistic behaviour. No wonder that Anton makes a plea that in consultancy work we should create a consultancy participant state of mind in all members of the organization. According to him, the most effective form of consultation would be a joint, systemic effort between staff and consultant at hypothesis-formation, subsequently putting these hypotheses to the test, and to continue to work together on their implementation.

In conclusion, in reflecting on the book, Anton makes it quite clear that the more we know, the better advice we can give. But it is oftentimes the case that the less we know, the more advice we tend to give. The wise man has his thoughts in his head, but it is the fool who expresses these thoughts with his tongue. Anton articulates strongly that the worst thing to do in organizations is not to do things wrongly but to do things for the wrong reasons. Workplace intelligence requires a solid comprehension of what's happening under the surface. Without it, organizational consultants, along with its members, will not be operating according their own agenda, but will be prey to the agenda of others.

Manfred Kets de Vries is the Distinguished Professor of Leadership Development and Organizational Change at INSEAD, Graduate Business School, the founder of INSEAD's Global Leadership Centre, and Programme Director of INSEAD's top management programme 'The Challenge of Leadership: Developing your Emotional Intelligence'.

Part I

The dynamics of human development

Introduction

This book is intended for all who perform a work leadership or management role, and also for those who, in turn, are led or managed in their professional life. Most of the ideas expressed, of course, also have relevance in one's personal or social life, but the main emphasis of this work is on managing oneself in role in the most constructive way – to self, to colleagues, to work. To adapt a Roman concept '*mens sana, in corpore sano, in corporation sana*' (a healthy mind, in a healthy body, in a healthy workplace). This work aims to be a bridge between the psychological approach to leadership that most people don't bother to engage with, it supposedly being 'too wet' and 'touchy feely', and the business school approach which is peppered with case studies that few people find easy to apply in their own back-home work setting.

Both approaches have their merits, but the risk is of being a zealot of one or other, rather than seeing matters from an overall 'ecological' perspective. Without anchoring one's approach in the personal experience of development, any system of relating to others is likely to be shallow and awkwardly artificial.

After much thought and discussion, I have settled on the title of the book as *Workplace Intelligence*. Intelligence, of course, has two meanings – in everyday language – it refers to information about the military environment, politics, and the views of others. Intelligence is also used to refer to the 'intellectual giftedness' of the person as measured in the Intelligence Quota (IQ). Later, the concept of emotional intelligence (EQ) developed, referring to the individual's capacity to relate to others and his/her surroundings. This required being in touch with self and others. Workplace intelligence is intended as a state of mind that applies the above two mentioned concepts to a third setting, namely the workplace.

Chapter 1

The terminology used

I use the term *organization* to describe the bricks and mortar and staff and equipment component of a boundaried group of individuals who have a common primary task. A factory, a school, a business, would be examples of such a structure.

I use the term *institution* to describe the state of mind or functioning of the organization. Institution would thus describe the organization's 'soft' conscious and unconscious working practices and beliefs.

I use the term *group* to describe a collection of individuals in pursuit of a common goal. Thus a dahlia-growing society might not have bricks and mortar and employees, but they would have a common goal – the study and growing of dahlias.

A transient collection of individuals in a restaurant or bus queue, by contrast, would not be seen as a group.

With organizations, institutions, and groups certain dynamics are inherent. An awareness and knowledge of these lay the foundations for what is going on, and to an extent why it happens. It thus helps to have a certain number of fundamental concepts to begin to understand the specific dynamics of what one is about to experience.

I use the term *observation* to mean a state of mind free of preconception – one of noting the behaviour and quality of the interactions and processes inherent in the functioning of the observed, whether concrete or symbolic, conscious or unconscious.

Chapter 2

The structure of this book

The book is divided into five parts. The first is about the ecology and dynamics of human development. The second is about the everyday dynamics of organizations – what is normal in the sense of institutional functioning, and, therefore, to be expected, and what is not within the norms of the everyday workplace. The third is about the connection between self and workplace dynamics and how these might be managed as member, as manager or leader, or as coach and consultant. The fourth is about practical and technical matters and the fifth about coaching, consultancy, and related matters.

In my attempt to make the book more sympathetic to its audience, I have committed two cardinal academic sins: no footnotes and no references, and one venal sin: no acknowledgements.

If you can't say it in the general communication you have in mind, it probably isn't worth the footnote. As regards references, they take up an awful lot of space and time in their creation, and anybody who really wants to follow-up an idea can nowadays find endless references on the internet.

As for acknowledgements, I am so indebted to a multitude of teachers, colleagues, patients, clients, that I cannot even get round to naming them all.

The book is an attempt to help create a symbolic tailored 'leadership suit' to your personal and organizational needs, rather than a garment that flops around you or is too constrictive and one-size-fits-all.

In creating the suit the first thing that needs to be taken into account is your body shape. No one in their right mind would assume that we all have the same body shape, yet in relation to work issues it is almost a given that we assume that everybody does, or should, see events the same way as we do. There is an assumption that we all have the identical 'mental shape' in seeing the world.

When it does become clear that, in fact, everyone has their own particular way of seeing things, we, as a result, are inclined to spend an inordinate amount of time trying to get others to see things our way rather than to freely consider their version of events. Not that either way is necessarily right or wrong – it is more a matter of keeping an open mind and being free to consider a variety of perspectives.

When it comes to bodies, it is fairly obvious as to what the determinants of our shape are – genetics, family history, diet (mental and physical), exercise, and culture. When it comes to our own states of mind, matters are a lot more complex. To understand how we come to have our particular emotional apparatus for seeing things, it is necessary to have some insight into how we got to be that way, how it affects our perception both consciously and unconsciously, and, therefore, how it affects us in our work and leadership roles. Having some understanding along these lines can contribute to understanding our strengths and weaknesses, and can protect us to a degree from a 'blind' and 'thoughtless' approach to life and work.

This, in turn, can facilitate us to create and maintain a more 'wholesome' work–life balance for us and for those around us. In doing so, we may also become better role models for those in both personal and work roles who, at least in part, model themselves on us.

Keeping an eye on understanding our own personal behaviour and reactions also puts us into a better position to 'put oneself into other people's shoes'. As a wise colleague of mine once said 'in order to put yourself into someone else's shoes, you have to take your own shoes off first'. So, hopefully, we now have a suit and shoes. The rest will follow with time.

Chapter 3

On observation

The basic approach of this book is based on observation of human behaviour in all its forms, at all ages, and in a variety of social and cultural settings. Following this the emphasis is on applying the above basic 'ecological' principles to application in our everyday professional conduct and procedures.

Perhaps the best illustration of the ecology approach is in agriculture. The maximum production approach totally ignores the ecology of local flora and fauna and turns the landscape into prairies doused with chemical fertilizers and pesticides. In the short term this produces maximum output; in the long term it destroys the natural ecosystem and makes the system less able to adapt to new circumstances. Symbolically, a non-ecological global management approach has the same results as in agriculture.

In pursuing the ecological metaphor, the most fruitful settings for observations are as follows:

1. The self and observing one's own feelings and reactions to the environment
2. Observing others in a variety of settings and the workplace – as mentioned, the observation needs to be as free as possible of one's own preconceptions
3. Forming a tentative hypothesis as to what is going on and what it means. However, you need to 'flirt with the hypothesis and not marry it'. The moment you do the latter you close down all other possibilities and blinker yourself
4. Plan a tentative intervention and observe the response
5. Continue with the cycle as above

This approach assumes that a great deal of learning is to be gained from observing how human beings deal with certain issues 'in nature' as it were, and to then see whether following the basic principles observed might lead to progress in addressing similar problems at another level of human functioning – specifically in professional and leadership roles.

A simple metaphor for this approach would be a 'Russian Doll'. All the dolls packed into each other are the same, but the sizes are different. The smallest doll might symbolize the individual or the individual's inner world make-up. The largest doll might represent society or the dynamics of the particular industry concerned. Intermediate dolls might represent subgroup, group, or inter-group representations.

The idea is that if one is stuck trying to understand the dynamic of one setting, for example, in a small work group, they can scale down the range of Russian Doll concepts, perhaps to the natural dynamic of a family group. In this way, one might reach a new understanding based on parallels between the family small group dynamics and the work group. This has the potential to shift the 'logjam' experienced and help to find a way ahead.

For example, one might again get in touch with the reality that rivalry and tension in family groups is a normal everyday event, and feel somewhat less surprised and annoyed that a similar dynamic might appear in a family-sized work group. A degree of perspective will thus have been gained that hopefully will somewhat defuse the tension and irritation of finding oneself in a 'dysfunctional' group. Dysfunction in a family group from time to time is a normal occurrence, just as it is in a small working group.

The point to be taken from the above example is that, if seen from a developmental (Russian Doll) perspective, the problem can be viewed and addressed from a more relaxed position than if it were viewed solely from a rigid management perspective. The latter view might be expressed as: small working groups should function well, and if they don't there is either something wrong with the group, its members (or more specifically one particular member), or with me in my membership/leadership role.

This may, of course, be partially or rarely even wholly true, but seeing it from only that perspective then leads to either 'bullying' the group into a pseudo-well-functioning mode, or else of scapegoating a member or self. Neither process makes for good ongoing institutional functioning.

Implied in the above approach is also the need to exercise the capacity to tolerate for some time a sense of uncertainty and of not knowing, instead of taking immediate flight into supposedly remedial action.

This book follows a human developmental pattern – what is to be learnt from basic human development from conception to death, and how these processes manifest themselves in our everyday personal and work settings. In work settings they would apply both in our role as managers and leaders, but also in being managed and led.

The view is that an approach based on observation and learning from experience makes for a more viable and realistic professional way ahead than one that is based on unrealistic ideals on the basis of wish-fulfilment or self-idealization.

Chapter 4

Your picture of the world and how it affects your work and personal life

One thinks one is in control of one's destiny, but, in fact, one is carried along by the stream.

To the unthinking this might appear to be another one of those frivolous philosophical fancies. In reality, it is a very insightful perspective on life, for it acknowledges that although consciously we believe that we are directly in charge of our lives – and thus of our personal and professional lives – that is only part of the story. This 'stream' is a key factor that influences our lives and the greater awareness we have of its ways, the greater our capacity to manage ourselves. Insight into the meanderings and attributes of the unconscious stream that carries us along is, therefore, a worthwhile quality to pursue; for example, a cox who understands where the current flows will know that sometimes cutting corners on a river and going the shortest route will, in fact, result in a slower time. This is because travelling with the current and using its power gives a distinct advantage. The key element of this unconscious stream that influences our life and conduct is not only that it affects the way we live our life, but, more importantly, that it influences how we see ourselves and, especially, how we see, judge, and manage others.

The unconscious stream thus operates as the equivalent of a lens (with all the accuracy as well as all the faults of such an optical apparatus) through which we see the world. How does the formation of this psychic lens happen? All parents will have noticed that each child's personality from birth onwards is different. Some are calm and innately content, others restless and miserable, and so on. This early behaviour is initially on account of inherited genetics, and there is also some recent evidence that intra-uterine and birth experience may play a part. Following that, the child interacts with its environment, and in so doing builds up an 'inner world' picture of the external world – initially, in relation to the mother or mothering function – and so on. There are obviously a multiplicity of factors that contribute to the picture, but the 'transitional' end result is that the child lays the foundation in its personality of the world and its inhabitants. It is this reality that makes for the essentials of the unconscious stream of perceptions and assumptions that carries us through life – the lens through which we see and evaluate the world and its inhabitants.

Example

If the inner world picture is one in which the world and its inhabitants is an uncaring place and that one had better look out for oneself because no one else will do so, this might very well function as an effective spur to becoming a 'self-made' entrepreneur, and a successful one at that. There may, however, be a personal price to pay, as one might not allow oneself to be cared for. A further downside may be running an organization in which care and support for others is seriously lacking, to the detriment of the organization. It is thus advisable in one's adult role to give some thought to how we came to be the way we are, and to use that insight to build on our strengths and assets, but also to keep an eye on our vulnerabilities – our 'Achilles Heel' emotionally speaking – and to do whatever we can to minimize the problem as it affects us and our personal and professional relationships. How to go about this will be addressed in later chapters.

Chapter 5

On beginnings

By definition, beginnings are the venues of hope and expectation. Without them, there would be little chance of change being embarked on. At the same time, it is clear that, if there is to be change, then at least some elements of the past have to be given up. These elements might be cherished ones or even previously complained about ones. No matter which applies there is always ambivalence about the process – one wishes for change or a new beginning; at the same time one does not wish for the disruption that such a process is feared to cause.

In embarking on a new beginning one also needs to face the element of uncertainty of what one is heading for. Moving forward into something of which one knows exactly what it is going to be like is either no change at all, or else is likely to be a denial of change and the beginning of something new – a state of mind which diminishes one's capacity to make the adaptations necessary to face the unknown and the process of change.

Going back to the Russian Doll image, the earliest human development example of change is probably pregnancy. There is a known period of 'incubation' of the idea and the reality of the baby that is likely to be met. There are various 'symptoms': feeling unwell, morning sickness, change of body shape, medical investigations, that all affect the previous state of mind of the mother, couple, and social system. Preparations need to be made, both emotionally and concretely in the form of equipment, for coping with the new arrival. In some instances, when there is undue anxiety or a previous miscarriage, preparations are partly or completely avoided until the child has arrived. The point made is that transition takes time and there is a need for incubation of thought and awareness of hopes and fears.

How does this relate to the topic of the book? The basic principle is that beginning, transition, and change needs time and thoughtfulness for it to be managed well, and for the individual and organization to be in touch with both the hopes and the fears evoked by the process.

Focussing solely on the hopes or the fears makes for a 'skewed' approach and gives the message that the 'other' half of the 'emotional equation', whether hopeful or hopeless, cannot be spoken or thought about. It is natural for there to be what one might call 'mood swings' about the matter of change, whether personal, work-related, or 'corporate'.

Focussing on only one parameter can happen, for example, in corporate mergers where the management focusses only on the positive aspects, presenting a so-called 'win–win' perspective, means that doubts, fears, or negativity are relegated to unofficial channels of gossip where they cannot be harnessed in the service of thought-through incubated change. The end result is that the process of change cannot be adequately dealt with because key elements become 'taboo' subjects not to be dealt with and, therefore, the end result is inevitably a skewed picture with a problematic outcome.

In reality, there are no win–win situations. The concept is, of course, nowadays a very popular one, especially amongst leaders who are the most likely to personally gain from the so-called benefits of a win–win situation. The concept of a win–win situation is also popular because it denies the presence of any negative effects or consequences of a so-called win–win implementation. Win–win is thus the institutional application of denial of the work required to deal with the process of addressing the picture as a whole – positives and negatives – and the ambivalence inherent in such work.

These matters apply not only to individuals making transitions and embarking on new beginnings, whether changing jobs or in existing jobs, moving to other sectors of the company or, as is common these days, being transferred to another global setting. The state of mind we are talking about affects not only the individual and her or his family, but also groups or branches of the company as they move about. It is by now well-known that a high percentage of so-called 'win–win' mergers do not succeed. It is, therefore, important to make allowance for time and transition, but equally important, it needs to be understood that to be able to 'put oneself into the shoes of the other' – in this case the 'newcomer' – is an essential part of the transition process for all concerned.

Chapter 6

On transference

It was Sigmund Freud who developed the idea of transference. Rather than being an exotic psychoanalytic term and concept, at best to be avoided, it is, in fact, an everyday useful idea applicable in all human relations. Its meaning is simple: if you are in a new situation, with little evidence of what is going on, you fall back on your past experiences and interpret what you see and experience in the here and now in terms of how you had experienced such matters in the past. So, in effect, you transfer your experience of the past to the present new situation, and judge the new according to past experience. This is an unconscious process.

If, for example, you had a tough early life with, as perceived by you, little external emotional and perhaps also concrete support, you will perceive a new situation in a similar light, misread the climate as fundamentally unsupportive and unfriendly, and continue with your 'self-made independent person' state of mind. In certain settings, at certain times, that might be of great benefit to you. If, however, you do not recognize that you have this quality-cum-blind spot, you might very well find yourself in personal, family, and work difficulties, with 360-degree feedback reports that you are poor at communicating, don't listen, and are not good at team relations. A resolve to alter this without recognition of the cause of such behaviour, and concern at the damage you are causing, is unlikely to be enough to change matters.

The essential feature of the transference concept is thus that your early personal experience in life causes you to see and interpret present-day life events through an unconscious emotional lens that influences and, in part, determines your perception. Unconscious here means that you are not aware that you are doing it, and assume that what you are seeing is 'reality'. It is, in fact, reality, but it is your specific psychic reality – it is not, as one assumes, the reality that everyone else also sees.

The core question here is thus whether one understands that one's personal lens has got both strengths that come from insight into the self, but also 'blind spots' that can seriously interfere with one's judgement. It is on account of this dynamic that psychoanalysts and psychotherapists have to undergo lengthy analysis themselves, in order to understand the clarities and distortions of their own psychic lens, lest they see their own faults in others. I am not suggesting that each and every manager should have an analysis, but I am suggesting that a degree of insight into one's strengths and weaknesses makes for better leadership. Getting feedback about oneself is an uncomfortable process. Ostensibly we all embrace and welcome feedback – the proviso is, however, that the feedback which is most welcome is the feedback that confirms our self-image. It is, therefore, not surprising that those in power frequently surround themselves with acolytes who shield them from reality. Nowadays feedback techniques are commonly used as part of staff reviews.

In 360-degree feedback situations, it is common to find defensive comments about the feedback from its recipients like 'oh – he's new and doesn't understand' or 'it's a cultural difference'. Comments of this kind are, at least in part, to be seen as defensive denial processes in order to keep one's self-image intact, avoiding any pain and necessary thoughtfulness of viewing the feedback implications.

When meeting with others, particularly in a leadership role, but also as a colleague, mentor or coach, it is helpful to also ask yourself: how does this person experience me? In other words, what is the nature of his or her personal lens, and how does this affect our working together?

Even though it may be a difficult question to answer the least one can do is to remind oneself that the way you see yourself is not necessarily the way others see you, as mentioned earlier. The way they see you is likely to be, at least in part, influenced by transference – that is, through the unconscious lens of their particular perception of you. It is also sobering to remember that they might very well see aspects of you that you yourself are perhaps in denial of, or blind to.

It is always important to keep in mind that no human interaction is free of at least some elements of this dynamic, in both directions, and that an awareness of it can help to diffuse difficult institutional work matters.

It is important to realize that being perceived by someone in a particular way is not only a matter of their perception of you; it is also a matter that being perceived, and, therefore, treated, in a particular way is an unconscious way of 'pushing you' into behaving in that manner, almost as a 'feedback loop'.

Example

If you are seen by somebody as a particularly kind leader you might very easily find yourself in a position of exercising kindness to a fault in relation to that person. This could result in a dynamic of crossing boundaries that transgress the work role and cause counterproductive group rivalries.

In a situation like this it is emotionally preferable to want to be 'loved' and to act accordingly. The danger, however, is that such behaviour risks the possibility of the primary task becoming one of 'needing to be loved' rather than conducting oneself in line with whatever is required of your role in the organization. The latter behaviour might well cause ambivalence but is more likely to generate respect of one's conduct in the role.

This process of transference is, of course, as mentioned, not a one-way matter, for the leader in this case would also have feelings towards the other. This counter-reaction is called counter-transference. A leader who, for example, was the eldest child in a family and who had a challenging younger sibling, might at times unconsciously fall into a state where there is some confusion about whether it is the member of staff being dealt with or the younger sibling. Putting down a younger sibling may have been appropriate; pouring cold water on the ideas of a new and/or younger member of staff may be less so, and deprive the organization of much-needed creativity.

How one is seen by others is not only a matter of individual perception. There is also the phenomenon of 'group' or 'institutional' transference, where, for example, a leader is perceived by a multitude of individual employees.

By this I mean an unconsciously held assumption of what one is like as an individual, but also, and more importantly, the perception of one in one's work role. In one's role as leader it is worthwhile giving some thought to this process, and to consider whether the perception and the resultant behaviour by the staff is in the service of the health and effectiveness of the organization, or not.

For example, an assumption that one is a penny-pinching micro-manager might save the pennies and cause staff to be meticulous in their behaviour, but that does not necessarily mean that the organization is functioning at its best, as growth, development, creativity, and innovation require a degree of investment and risk taking.

Chapter 7

On joining a 'new' organization

We are not in a position to know how it feels to the newborn to come into the world, and thereby join his or her new organization – the mother, parents, family. However, we are able to observe the effect on existing members of the organization/family of the arrival of the newcomer.

The process starts long before the actual arrival/birth when unconscious fantasies are explored or, for that matter, denied about what the newcomer is likely to be like. The usual parental response is to present the occasion as an overwhelmingly joyous event, while doubts and negativity are generally repressed – confined to bad dreams and nightmares. Many of us will have had the experience of witnessing the reaction of an older child to the arrival of a baby. This may take the form of transient interest followed by an enquiry into when the new infant would be taken back to – and left at – the hospital. Conversely, it may involve loving it so hard that the parent has to *save* the baby from the sibling's suffocating embrace.

With close observation, it must also be noticed that it is not only the siblings that are affected. Fathers, too, feel excluded, especially if the 'sibling feelings' of their own past are re-ignited, and even the family dog can be seen to fall into a 'miffed', excluded state of mind while some cats leave home entirely. Such responses are normal, and hopefully, with time, the family reaches an accommodation. Yet sometimes one comes across cases of families in which an older sibling has never, in years, mentioned the name of the newcomer!

So what does this have to do with the process of beginnings and of managing oneself, as follower or leader, or both, in an organization? Fast forward a few Russian Dolls, and you will find that the same processes of anticipation mixed with negative feelings are swishing about in the organization/institution. Although the effect will be much more noticeable in a smaller group than in a large organization, large organizations are, nonetheless, made up of smaller subsets, and it is in these that the aforementioned dynamics are enacted.

For the existing resident work group members, the question arises of how the arrival of the newcomer will affect the existing group dynamics. On the one hand, there is perhaps the dynamic of looking forward to the arrival of the new appointee who, it is hoped, will ease the workload of the others in some area or another.

On the other hand, it raises the frightening question of whether one's own position will be threatened. This is not with regard to the official job description of one's role relative to others, but to the unconscious and unspoken 'pecking order' of the existing work group.

Consciously one would assume that the existing group would be welcoming and supportive of the newcomer; helping them over time to find their feet. No doubt this happens to some degree in all new appointments, but that is not the problem. Rather, problems arise with the occurrence and enactment of negative feelings about the new arrival.

Commonly, very little time and effort is spent on helping newcomers to settle in. Often it amounts to no more than a 'guided tour' of the facilities, and the newcomer is then left to find their own way. This lack of support may be due to unspoken negative feelings about the new appointee, along the lines of 'they'll have to learn the hard way how to cope here – just as I had to'. Traditionally, this dynamic can be found in traditional old English boarding schools wherein a cut off state of mind was encouraged in order to survive the depression, isolation, and loneliness. Family, friends, and colleagues may later pay the price.

Example

A national grocery chain had a major supply problem. Instead of crates of tinned tomatoes arriving, as ordered, tinned fish arrived instead, and so on. It turned out that the company had a 'fast track' manager recruitment programme under which so-called bright graduates were hired and put through a six-month 'company acclimatisation programme' that involved working their way through all departments. It is not difficult to imagine the response to these bright young sparks from the old forklift truck drivers and staff in the warehouses. Unsurprisingly, it gave them pleasure to see the young stars make a mess of things, gratifying the existing staff's unconscious wish for an envious attack on these 'golden youngsters'. Sabotage can take a conscious or unconscious form.

One must keep in mind that it is common for new recruits of this kind to come into the organization with the state of mind of being 'special', and, therefore, of not needing to learn from the 'old hands'. Likewise, the 'old hands' response to the new *wunderkinder* is not unique. Nor is the resulting *schadenfreude* – German for pleasure at the misfortune befalling others – a surprise.

In this instance, what was particularly problematic was that the 'normal' interaction was not foreseen, and thus no measures were put in place to allow both parties to cooperate and learn from the experience. It is not beyond possibility that the newcomers might have learnt a lot from the 'old hands', not only about forklift trucks and warehousing, but also about company assumptions and morale. And the newcomers might very well have spotted some existing practices that deserved questioning, or come up with ideas that merited consideration by existing staff.

In crossing the boundary into a new role or organization, there is always the need for adjustment. Usually, the assumption is that the newcomer must, and should, adjust to the existing in-house ways of doing things. This is a reasonable expectation, and if that were not the case then the organization would soon fall into disorganization and chaos. Nonetheless, there is a matter of degree. In armies, for example, recruits are stripped of all personal identity, clothes, haircut, and more, and are turned into numbers. This is regarded as necessary for an effective top-down managed system.

Whether the same process is necessary for new recruits into an organization is questionable. For a start, all recruits bring with them personal experience as well as expertise in the field to which they are appointed, and often related areas. Treating them as if they were 'virginal' in all respects may well be more comfortable for the company joined, but means that a potential wealth of experience that could easily be relevant to the new position – and the future of the organization – is at risk of being ignored and lost.

Example

A teacher with years of experience in problematic classes decides to become an insurance salesperson. One might argue that she/he needs to completely retrain in order to understand the insurance market. That undoubtedly is true – but what about the years of experience of dealing with individuals who don't, or only partially, listen to what is said by the teacher/salesperson?

The risk to both parties, new and existing, is as follows:

The newcomer presents him/herself as an empty vessel free of experience and thought. The organization fills the empty vessel with 'how things are done here'. Both parties find this 'comfortable'. There is little questioning, and not much upset on either side.

Newcomers who don't go along with this approach are at risk of being seen as poor appointments or misfits. By contrast, those who fully comply are seen as good appointments. The organizational status quo is kept and the newcomer is effectively institutionalized.

The problem illustrated above is that the past experience of the newcomer is lost. Particularly important is that element of the newcomer that has the ability to see elements of institutional functioning that might be questioned or modified, perhaps with a 'fresh set of eyes'. There is thus a loss of creativity to the organization – a loss that it can ill afford.

Resistance to new ideas, and the fate of those who question existing ideas, is well documented in history.

Example

Galileo Galilei (1564–1642) was an Italian physicist, mathematician, astronomer and philosopher who played a major role in the scientific revolution. Galileo questioned the geo-centric view that the earth was the centre of the universe. For questioning this utterly accepted view, he was denounced to the Church, tried, and found 'vehemently suspect of heresy'. Galileo was forced to recant and spent the rest of his life under house arrest.

I am not suggesting that there are many Galileos amongst new appointees, or that existing organizations are as out of touch with 'reality' as the Church at that time was in relation to astronomy – but it is worth keeping an eye open for new ideas that might creep through the tiniest chinks in institutional functioning, and open up new opportunities for growth and development.

It is also worth keeping in mind the fairy tale of the 'Emperor's New Clothes':

> the Emperor was vain and so when some chancers appeared at court offering to make him the most fabulous set of clothes on earth he succumbed. The charlatans tapped him for enormous

sums to purchase gold and silver and other materials for the outfit. From time to time, the Emperor sent court members to observe the progress of the project. The courtiers became caught up in the madness and feared for their lives if they were to reveal the truth – that the whole operation was a scam. Instead, they came back with glowing reports of progress. Finally the Emperor decided to put on his new clothes and to appear in public. The populace were 'enchanted' and praised the Emperor for his garments. Only one little boy in the crowd spoke up with, 'but he's naked!' This boy was clearly the sole member of the population who was not caught up in the mass hysteria and group state of mind and stated the reality. The same dynamic, albeit to a lesser degree, happens in organizations that delude themselves. Think only of the fate of whistleblowers and how regularly they are denigrated.

Chapter 8

On anxiety in the workplace

The notion of anxiety is by no means an everyday management concept addressed in business school or top peer-reviewed management journals. If, however, there is truth in the saying that 'the child is father to the man' then the situation looks somewhat different.

Observe a young child hopping along the pavement in a peculiar way. If we look in greater detail, the child is hopping from paving-stone to paving-stone, avoiding the cracks. When asked why, you would usually get a nonchalant answer, 'because', 'for fun', etc. Dig deeper, and you might be initiated into the thought that the child does not want to fall into the cracks that are felt to be infinitely deep. Another child taps every second lamp post – 'to ward off evil spirits'. Some adults won't walk under ladders; others fear meeting a black cat crossing the road. Some 'touch wood', others believe in secret numbers. Some hotels don't have room no. 13, and many airlines go straight from 12 to 14 when naming seat rows. What are these rituals about? Surely not logic. They are instead the tip of the iceberg of underlying primitive anxieties the unconscious 'groundwater' that we are all subject to.

Parents have all observed one or other child having a favourite soft toy or rag doll, or even rag, that is an essential companion for that child, and which no parent would risk leaving behind – or perhaps even washing – for fear of the consequent distress to the child. Some of these objects accompany individuals at least into adult life, others forever. In the army, they take the form of regimental mascots. In London, they take the form of the ravens at the Tower of London. In Gibraltar, the apes on the Rock.

The function of these primitive rituals and objects is to keep at bay primitive anxieties. If the rituals are not followed, we fear that something unfortunate, if not catastrophic, might befall us. Consciously, we all know that such behaviour is nonsense. Yet nevertheless, many of us indulge 'just in case'. We do not want to provoke the Gods.

The easy way out of thinking (and respecting) such processes is to pretend that we all have 'outgrown' such primitive childhood thinking. In reality, that is not the case – our earlier 'primitive' self remains an integral part of our identity even though it is encased in a 'veneer' of 'grown-upness'. When times get tough our 'inner core dynamics' influence our adult decisions.

How does this affect our everyday work roles and, furthermore, why should such matters have any significance for us at all?

For a start, an awareness of such matters means that we can keep an eye open, and avoid causing offence by blindly stamping on or infringing, with harmless practices and rituals that are, perhaps, of crucial importance to the people practising them.

A consultant colleague of mine, who did a study of the rituals practised by the inhabitants of the Andaman Islands, reported that if one yawned one immediately had to click one's fingers in front of one's open mouth in order to prevent 'bad spirits' entering one's body.

One could think of religious rituals. But more immediately, and less speculatively, it is worth looking at the many practices in our organizations that might also have a partly, or wholly, ritualistic function along the lines stated above. In wishing to effect change it might be worth considering that seemingly irrelevant practices, if tampered with unthinkingly, might be the tip of the iceberg of unconscious processes, and thus of much greater consequence than would initially appear.

Apart from the 'unconscious groundwater' described, in all of us and in our organizations, there are also 'industry-specific' anxieties. For example, in the nuclear, chemical, and petrochemical industries anxieties will feature explosions, disaster, and catastrophe; in healthcare, they are about dying and death. In fact, many of our social systems, whether health, education, the police, prisons, the army, could be seen as social systems to deal with various social needs and requirements. This includes the protection from certain anxieties that the systems are there to contain. Health systems based on earlier Shaman, Witch-doctor, Holy Man systems survive to intervene on our behalf against death; the police are there as a shield between us and rampant violence; the army as a way of structuring and containing murderousness.

Example

On a more practical note, take the petrochemical industry. For everyone, from the simplest cleaner to the chief executive, it is essential to be in touch with the risks of their business. The Bhopal chemical disaster of 1984 in India is a sobering example of what can happen when this is not the case. In short, the report into the disaster stated that many had noticed the build-up of problems, but the safety function had been delegated to one team. This meant that no one else took responsibility and turned a blind eye. And the rest is history.

If one works in a 'dangerous' industry, it is emotionally tiring, overwhelming even, to keep on reminding oneself, or to be reminded, of the everyday, or for that matter, the minute-by-minute risks with which one is living. It is much easier, and quite understandable, to fall into a state of 'turning a blind eye' to the issues, or fall into a state of denial concerning the risks. It is easier on the self and more 'comfortable' for the organization. It is also increasingly a denial of the fact that one is sitting on a disaster waiting to happen. If everyone takes this stance towards the risk, the chances are high that, eventually, a disaster *will* happen.

Denying the risk, and falling into a defensive state of mind against being in touch with the anxiety, is thus highly counterproductive in relation to good management; it can also turn out to be financially hugely expensive and a public relations disaster.

The basic principle that arises from this level of anxiety is that there needs to be sufficient ongoing awareness of the risks and anxieties associated with the business that one is engaged in.

Given the present-day awareness of global ecology, the days are over of proceeding with one's everyday industrial processes with hardly a thought about the consequences for 'mother earth'. All organizations and industries have an ecological footprint. Given the recent shift from a 'community employer' to a 'local polluter' status, it is not surprising that organizations are defensive and, in part, in denial about the effect they are having on the environment. Furthermore, there is the everyday psychological development relating to 'truth-telling' in society.

Example

There is a crashing sound in the kitchen; mother's favourite china cup is in pieces on the floor and the nearby 3-year-old says 'teddy bear did it'. The child had not yet learnt that which a British diplomat recently blandly described in an interview as 'being economical with the truth'.

We all, to one degree or another, learn in our development to be economical with the truth. At times it serves a useful purpose, shielding individual or organization from humiliation and worse.

But there is also an extremely negative consequence of this behaviour. If we cannot be open about certain issues and facts it means that we cannot work at addressing them. Subsequently, the problem becomes more and more entrenched, more and more denied, and thus eventually much harder to address.

Openness about the existence of the problem, even if there is no immediate or even eventual solution in sight, at least means that, with time and thought, various ways of chipping at and addressing aspects of it might become available. This would eventually lead to a diminution, if not a resolution, of the problem. The recent development of Schwartz Rounds following increased openness in the airline industry goes some way to address these issues.

Any organization that states that we have no such problems, or we have solved all problems, is not one that should be given a 'gold star of merit'. Instead, it should be recognized that the organization is in a state of denial, and has not put into place the necessary mechanisms to be open and to address ecological problems as they arise.

Chapter 9

Personal manifestations of anxiety

Anxiety is likely to arise in individuals working in the 'people industries' – hospitals, social services departments, the police, the fire bri-
gade, schools, prisons, the voluntary sector, etc. In these professions,
the requirements of the 'client groups' are particularly emotionally
loaded.

It might be interesting to note that a disproportionate number of
staff working with children in care grew up in care homes themselves. One could say that this is understandable; they are trying to
make lives better for those on the same difficult life path that they
themselves followed. One would hope that their personal life experience would make them more sympathetic to the problems of their
clients, and, therefore, in a better position to help them address these
problems.

This may, indeed, be the case. However, there is another side to the
equation. Having had similar experiences to those of their clients –
experiences that they themselves have perhaps only partially or su-
perficially overcome – they are more vulnerable to the onslaught of
problems presented to them by their charges, and this then puts them
at risk of their professional competence being undermined.

Human development can be perceived as a pathway on which a
variety of obstacles and challenges must be overcome. In the early
stages, these are issues like trust, dependence and independence, and
so on. At each stage, the issue is mastered, hopefully to a satisfactory
or 'good enough' degree. Matters that remain unresolved are carried along in the developmental stream, with opportunities arising at
later development stages to have 'another go' at resolution.

The 'undealt' with aspects get carried along as well, and are often carried on in an 'encapsulated' sort of way. They are present,
but don't necessarily have an everyday effect on the individual's life;

they are emotionally 'walled off'. They do, however, constitute the emotional equivalent of an inner world Achilles Heel or 'minefield'. Thus specific emotional outer world stimuli can, in effect, 'detonate' these enclaves and cause a breakdown of adult personal or professional behaviour.

Example

A social worker has an unresolved 'deprived baby' aspect of herself in her encapsulated inner world. When faced with a miserable, 'deprived, crying baby' client, she finds herself with *two* crying babies: one the client, the second the memory aroused within herself. The situation becomes unbearable, her professional stance is lost, and the client is turned to with anger and brutality to shut them up.

In turn, this struggle to keep oneself in an adequate professional state of mind, while keeping at bay both personal and work-related inner world pressures and anxieties, can eventually lead to what is popularly known as 'burnout'. In this state of mind, the individual concerned becomes essentially defensive, stuck, and dull in relation to work. Sadly, this state of affairs also often crosses into the broader world of the individual, affecting their personal life, their family, and social relationships.

What is lost is a sense of perspectives of energy and, more specifically, a sense of freedom and creativity. Work thus becomes routine and bureaucratic – a handicap not only to the individual's work, but also to the organization.

Example

A professor, year on year, gives the same lecture on the same subject to generations of students. The lecture might be good but the professor is at risk of becoming a victim of professional burnout.

The matter of personal emotional enclaves bringing with them risks and problems is, as mentioned, perhaps of particular relevance in the helping professions, but it is also worthwhile considering the effect of this type of dynamic in an everyday work context in all settings.

Chapter 10

Work manifestations of anxiety

Just as there are personal anxieties which are part of one's inner and outer world manifestations, so there are institutional anxieties arising from the nature of the work in which the institution and the industry are engaged. Some are obvious: the nuclear or petrochemical industries, as mentioned previously; while others, though less immediately present are nevertheless powerful influences in one's personal work life.

Example

At an evening social event for those in the legal profession, a senior member states that he is quite unaffected by the work and the decisions he has to make about his clients on a daily basis. 'Nonsense' interrupts his wife – 'when you've had a bad day even the family dog runs for the bushes'. This is an example of someone completely out of touch with the pressures of everyday work life.

The solution is not to be *fully* immersed in the emotional dynamics of the work, but to be at least partially in touch with its pressures. The judicial system, for example, has devised a series of rituals and dress to soften the person to person impact of the work. Again, these dynamics are particularly present in the 'people professions' but occur in all human activities. It is a wise individual who allows him or herself to identify, and be consistently 'in touch' with, the problematic and stressful elements of one's work.

There are also related 'softer' factors. The following is a useful metaphor for these:

Oceanographers and marine biologists have now established that all flotsam and jetsam in the oceans eventually breaks down into microscopic fragments that end up at the bottom of the oceans. Here, they mix with the natural plankton: contaminating and poisoning the natural ecology at the depths of the oceans. If seen symbolically, 'undealt with' and 'unthought about' mental and work issues, too, can 'sink to the bottom' of the mental space and become the equivalent of the poison contaminating the natural mental processes needed to 'clear the mental decks'.

Another model would be diesel particulates and the way in which they clog up our lungs and the atmosphere, despite being invisible. Is it too far-fetched to consider that unthought-through mental debris, arising from our work, can clog up our normal everyday mental cleansing systems? Is this part what happens in burnout? Our mental filters get clogged up? If so, what can be done about it? Be alert to the fact that there are also often unspoken problematic issues. Keeping an eye open for them – doing the best one can to minimize their noxious effect – can at least go some way to improving matters and clearing one's mind.

It also needs to be understood that the above-described dynamic affects not only the staff and the functioning of the institution, but also directly affects the state of the mind of the consumers/clients of the service. As a result, they may be less available to participate in an effective adult co-workership, and instead fall into a passive, dependent state of mind.

Part 2

The everyday dynamics of organizations

The everyday dynamics of organizations

Chapter 11

On change and resistance to change

We can cope with being ourselves. Uncomfortable as that might, at times, be, at least we know where we stand. With change, we enter an area of uncertainty; a new, different, and not previously managed uncomfortableness. Hence our resistance.

Change means having to cope with the experience of confusion, of giving up the certainty, or, more accurately, the pseudo-certainty of the past. It means unlearning: giving up ideas of the past and taking onboard new ideas about which we are unsure.

In the field of child development, you couldn't have a nicer example than the conversation between a child and an adult on the question of 'where babies come from'. If we leave aside the usual avoidance stories of storks or birds and bees, and explain to the child how babies are made, grow, and are born, they might listen to the facts with apt interest. A few days later they might very well have reverted to their old theories about the process – oral ingestion, storks, or magic. The reality is just too much to cope with at that moment.

Adults too, prefer to stick to their own view of the way things work. The same mechanisms of denial regularly occur, and, as with children, it often takes a long time for the true facts to sink in.

When struggling with the issue of having to accommodate to new facts or different ways of seeing things, it is not unusual for the individual, or for that matter the institution, to seek out other 'like-minded' individuals and to use them to bolster our defences against change. As part of this group dynamic it is often the case that the 'friends' recognize what it is that is emotionally and unconsciously required of them, and they thus, as it were, 'produce the necessary', in the service of denial.

This particular dynamic occurs at all levels of human interaction. It is, perhaps, most clearly evidenced in societies where the leader is increasingly surrounded by acolytes who confirm the perceptions of 'the great leader', and where anybody that questions these processes is seen as an enemy or traitor.

We are not speaking of 'rogue states', but, rather, how difficult it is for so-called 'whistleblowers' to be heard and how badly they are generally treated.

It should be understood that in order to develop an identity of self, whether personally or organizationally, it is important to have 'others'. Psychically, the simplest form of 'other' is an 'enemy'.

In its early developmental stages, the identity of the individual is shaped by a combination of genetic make-up and the family and wider social dynamics in which they find themselves. These early processes imply a degree of acceptance of the status quo. As adolescence is embarked upon, with all its hormonal drives, this is challenged and altered.

It is at this point that they begin to form an adult identity. The individual concerned is often in a state of crisis as to who they are: their individual and sexual identity, etc. This is dealt with through a process of relating to others with similar states of mind and problems and, perhaps more importantly, building an identity based on 'not being like others'. Often this refers to parents or individuals from older generations. Being like 'them' is considered to be a horror. The adolescents do not know who they are, but they are absolutely clear who they are not. This provides the security of having an identity, albeit one based on problematic grounds. With time, the boundary between the adolescent and the 'thems' becomes more permeable, and the need to have enemies in order to have an identity is diminished.

The enemy also serves the useful function of being a dumping ground for all sorts of personal negative qualities. These are difficult to deal with within oneself, and, therefore, one prefers to see them in others instead. This dynamic is clearly found in religious, racial, and other prejudices where, for example, 'God is on our side and the others are the Devil's spawn'. And it is the essential ingredient of jokes about other groups, professions, or nations.

These dynamics also exist in group situations, whether personal or work-related. They occur between departments of the same organization, and between competitor firms. 'We are an ethical and reliable firm making a good product – they are fly-by-night producers of poor quality goods'.

In a state of mind of self-idealization and of the denigration of others, there is a price to be paid: one loses touch with reality. It is, therefore, difficult to deal with any related issues and to update one's work functioning accordingly.

The above description of human development is based on an essentially 'western family' style of behaviour. In other cultures, development takes its own particular pathway. Nonetheless, within western societies there are also widespread differences in approach.

These differences also manifest themselves in the work processes of organizations in specific cultures. With the increase in multinational and global concerns, it is essential that some thought is given to how these processes affect multidisciplinary teams in the workplace, and, also, how the resulting 'cultural transplantations' affect individuals and their families.

The initial response to transplantation is to behave as before – as though nothing has changed – in one's previous social or work climate. This is a case of 'sticking with the known' that one has learnt to manage, and, in part, is an understandable process of denial of the new situation.

This denial is a reaction to the part-realization that much has changed, and that a substantial re-alignment with its accompanying anxiety is required.

The next step is thus to find like-minded individuals with whom one can build an enclave of 'usness'. These enclaves are often concrete, gated developments in which 'usness' is encouraged and 'otherness' is outside the boundary walls. While these walls may be of a symbolic nature, there are often real, concrete walls also in place. The 'others' outside might collude with this process as, for them, having to accommodate otherness is a threat to their own established lifestyle. This may or may not, depending on the circumstances, be the most appropriate way of beginning to live in a 'foreign' country. Interestingly, it is often the children of relocation who act as bridging agents between the enclave and the outside world.

In the global workplace, however, such 'enclavisation', if one might call it that, makes for substantial difficulty as regards the work of the organization. Having to relate to 'foreigners' with their 'foreign' ways of managing and thinking about issues can be a tiring, depressing process for all parties concerned. It is, however, as nothing compared to the consequences of not working with each other.

What is, therefore, required of all is the patience to sit down with each other and, on a regular basis, to observe other social, mental, and work attitudes. Then, one can discuss how they might affect workplace processes and routines. This is not about being 'missionaries' on a campaign to educate the 'natives', whomever the missionaries or the natives might be in any given scenario. Instead, I suggest a process of providing a thoughtful space in which observation of the other and their way working is open for discussion and evaluation. Arising from this process the hope is that some agreed way of proceeding is arrived at. The process is available for constant observation and open for modification as learning is applied. As described previously, this learning process is not without its problems, for it means that all concerned need to have a certain capacity to give up their cherished views on the way business should be done, and have an open mind for trying the unfamiliar.

It must be remembered that this manner of work is not only about difficulty, but if successful, can create a climate of goodwill that is welcome not only in terms of work morale but potentially resulting in financial rewards.

The difficulty of embarking on such a process of learning from each other, and then of embarking, in a modified way, on a common task, has a further problematic component. In training for our professional roles we learn the 'correct' way of going about things. This training often also takes the form of learning at 'the feet of our masters' who act as conscious and unconscious role models. The problem, as one can imagine, is that the 'correct way' in one society is not the same 'correct way' in another society, or in another age. In fact, it is often the incorrect way.

I distinctly remember a school parents' evening feedback from a mathematics teacher who said about my daughter, 'she always gets the correct answer but goes about it the wrong way!' We experience pressure to do things the 'correct way' – as we have been taught – from both societal and inner world allegiances.

Finding an accommodation using the above-described processes, means branching out for oneself, having one's own ideas, and abandoning, or at least modifying, the 'tablets of truth' handed down to us by our elders. That might be manageable. But in working in the global system, say, as a relocated engineer in China, one is likely, at some point, to be transferred back to one's native Finland. There, one finds that one's working practices as modified in China are out of kilter with the approach of one's ex-colleagues back home. One is thus at risk of being perceived by his or her fellow countrymen as 'having picked up foreign habits'. The required adaptation has to be dealt with, but it makes for additional work. Perhaps it is not that different from what the children have to cope with when they move from an 'international school' in China to the local high school in Finland. In effect, one could say that 'picking up foreign habits' is essential for survival and success in the present global economic system. This is something that the partners and dependents of those transferred need to learn and it can make for hard-to-bear stress on their parts.

What is regarded as an appropriate work–life balance is also a matter of cultural assumption and varies widely. Practices seen as normal in Japan might be regarded as exceptional elsewhere. It is understandable that individuals would wish to, and are under pressure to, conform to the work patterns inherent in their culture. If the workforce is multicultural and functioning in a global context, the need arises for a compromise to be reached that accommodates local culture while taking into account the global context of the company.

Chapter 12

On institutional functioning

In any organization there are two layers of functioning. On the surface there is the overt, conscious, official layer. This consists of management structures and roles, of mission statements, annual reports, and strategic plans, and so on. They all give an indication of the 'public face' the organization and its office bearers want to present. This layer is important and needs to be taken seriously, but it would be a mistake to think that this is the whole picture. Sometimes we get an honest take; sometimes there is covert – or overt – deceit.

The other side of the coin is the covert picture. How the power structures really function, who can 'fix things', whom to avoid, etc. And with this goes the question of group dynamics, both conscious and unconscious. The conscious group dynamic in, for example, a management group of eight, revolves around the roles of those sitting around the table: chief executive, chief operating officer, directors of finance, production, sales, etc. These individuals are there in their professional capacity and are expected to behave and respond accordingly to work issues in their sectors of responsibility and overall.

But when managing such a group, or being a member, or occasionally attending, it is important to understand the parallel existence of another – an unconscious – group dynamic. This refers to what, in addition to the above-mentioned concrete roles, individuals unconsciously bring and enact around the very same table.

First, there are the more obvious issues: gender, age, and experience in the company, race, pecking order amongst the members. Then there are the 'personality' components. The quiet one; the one who dominates and goes on endlessly; the robust one; the frail one; the star; the positive acolyte; the depressed, negative one. These roles are mostly determined by a combination of personality and group process.

This unconscious group layer and its resulting processes can often determine the outcome of meetings – more so than the first layer. What needs to be taken into account is that decisions disproportionately influenced by the second layer are often not task orientated, and have more to do with placating group dynamics than with addressing the decisions required for the continuation of the work and, therefore, the survival of the organization in a competitive world.

The group roles that individuals unconsciously enact in this 'second layer' dynamic are, as described, partly determined by the individual's personality and partly by the overall unconscious group process. By this, I mean that the group 'needs' certain functions to be represented. An example would be the 'mindless' supporter of the chief executive who in being 'mindless', i.e. without a personal opinion, always echoes the views of the chief executive. This might (or might not) be appreciated by the chief executive, but can cause as much institutional damage as the committee member who is always negative, about and against, whatever is proposed. The sort of person who, when he speaks, causes all others to raise their eyes to heaven, or, quietly, signal to the chief executive that he/she in no way speaks for them.

An awareness of the everyday occurrence of these dynamics is essential for reasons I shall lay out below.

For the leader, it is essential to understand that such dynamics are normal and an everyday event, though, of course, there is a question of the degree to which these behaviours manifest themselves. This perspective is counter to the alternative view that the above group is a particularly ill-functioning unit that one has assembled or been saddled with, or that the behaviour outlined is due to incompetence on one's part as a leader. All of the above might be true, but it is usually more helpful to give thought to how this state, in general, has come about, and what might be done about it.

Understanding the above – namely the 'normality' of such behaviour – puts the leader into a freer state of mind when addressing the issues and getting on with the business of the group. Interestingly enough, it should be noted that if there is a group in which none of the above-described dynamics ever occur, it is more than likely that such problematic elements are 'suppressed' in the group and instead 'leak out' in other settings. While that might feel more comfortable for the management group and its members, it means that the issues that 'leak out' in other settings are not available for discussion. Allowing dissatisfaction to fester amongst the ranks by a process of denial is not a good way of managing an organization.

Apart from the leadership perspective on the above-mentioned group processes, it is also important to understand that individual comments need to be understood, not solely as individual comments due to some or other individual personality quirks, but also as un-conscious contributions from the group as a whole about matters which affect all members of the institution.

Example

In the 19th century the most important 'member' of a coal-mining team was the pit canary. The bird was taken with the mining team in its cage to the coalface. If, and when, the pit canary keeled over, it was time to get out. This was because canaries were found to be much more sensitive to methane gas (an explosive gas found in coal seams) than human beings, and when the bird keeled over it was time for the mining team to evacuate the coal face.

The pit canary was thus the 'member' of the mining team most sensitive to a 'dynamic' affecting all members of the team. Equally 'Fred', the 'pain in the backside' member of the group, can, and should, be seen as the pit canary of, say, the management group. When Fred does his usual negative rant about something, and all others in the group cast their eyes to heaven disowning him, it is important not to write this off as a personal foible of Fred's, and to quietly engage in the planning of having him fired, but to consider whether he is bringing to the table a question of doubt about the proposal on the table – a question that needs to be taken seriously, and that needs to be addressed in spite of the ruction and discomfort this may cause to those others of the group who prefer that aspect of their judgement to be aired by Fred, leaving them free of con-tention and ambivalence. A wise chairman might deal with this by, perhaps, saying something along the lines of 'thank you Fred for that contribution – I'm sure that it is not only Fred who has some doubts about the project. Let us all openly address the issue and see what we might make of it'.

The technical assumption is thus that 'Fred' has, compared to other members of the group, a particular 'valency' (a term borrowed from science by the psychoanalyst Wilfred Bion) for certain issues of sensitivity. The other members of the group are either unaware or suppressing their equivalent thoughts or, to use a psychological term, 'projecting' this element into 'Fred'. 'Fred' thus has his own feeling, while at the same time acting as the unconscious 'Trojan Horse' for the others.

As a participating member of such a group it is important to ask oneself:

> what unconscious role do I play in the group? What slot have I been drafted into or made myself available for? Is this good for me personally, for me in my professional role, and also for the functioning of the group or not? And, in all circumstances what, if anything, can or should I do about it?

As for the question of 'what slot am I likely to fill, or unconsciously put myself forward for?' – the answer is simple. It is, in all likelihood, the slot that you traditionally put yourself forward for in all of your life: the slot and unconscious role that you have polished and perfected over the years, from when you were a small child, on through adolescence, adulthood, and your career, to the present day. The charmer, the helpful one, the rebel, the star, the doubting Thomas (Fred), etc. The issue is not that you should not be who you are. The issue is that an *awareness* of how you are likely to be in a group situation would help you to avoid falling into behaviour that might be detrimental to you and to what you are trying to achieve at that moment. As Denis Healey, the British politician, once said, 'when you're in a hole stop digging'. It is unlikely that you can put a complete stop to personal behaviour that you might wish to desist from, but with awareness and determination you might create a shallower hole and get out more quickly than before.

I do not wish to give the impression that groups are necessarily dangerous places, or that group processes can be avoided, but a degree of awareness of the existence and dynamic of such processes can make the difference between relative success and relative failure.

My core concept in these pages has been that of observation: observation and thought, and time for thought, before action. This seems a simple, if not naïve, approach. But there is ample evidence that leaders are under constant and relentless pressure to *act*, to be seen to be acting, and to act immediately and decisively. Such action can be perceived as impressive leadership, irrespective of whether the action is effective or not, and evidence-based or not.

An observation-based leadership approach is of necessity slower and, therefore, risks being seen as dithering and indecisive, particularly by those advocating a macho style of leadership. However, in all likelihood, it is more effective in the longer term. Placing observation and thoughtfulness at the centre of the leadership approach has certain key implications for both the leader and the organization. Primarily, it means that the leader has the capacity not to be immediately stampeded into a 'here and now decision', but to create a space for observation, reflection, and thought as to the way ahead – a space that includes and involves relevant others. This is not easily done, for most, if not all, decisions to be made come packaged in an envelope of anxiety. We feel: 'something has to be done now, and has to be seen to be done'. Such is the nature of the primitive unconscious anxiety in all individuals or organizations. This is the nature of the institutional anxiety in all of us.

All decisions thus come, at least in part, with an anxiety that something needs to be done urgently lest something dreadful befall us. In reality, in almost all cases, that is not the case, and there is time for observation, a gathering of facts, and decision-making. But it does not feel like that.

Why not? First, I think it is because very often decisions need to be made about matters in which the way ahead is unclear. If what needs to be done is clear, no 'decision' in an emotional sense needs to be made. Because this is a difficult and anxiety-inducing process, it is often avoided and, to use a metaphor, 'the issue is kicked into the long grass'. Or, for example, in the political realm, a committee might be appointed to look into the matter, and, by implication, to report back at a time when its findings will receive the least possible attention.

This process of avoiding decision-making is universal – if and when the problem does surface *again* and needs addressing, it often comes, as mentioned, packaged with a degree of urgency. The degree of urgency, caused by the delay in decision-making and given the unconscious 'groundwater' charge as described above, does thus sometimes make for a realistic sense of emergency, but never to the degree as experienced at the 'hot moment'. Examples of this are often experienced by external consultants who are called in at such hot moments.

Example

In the first session of a coaching consultancy meeting, the consultant finds himself or herself under increasing pressure to come up with an immediate solution to the problem posed by the client, the chief executive of a large company. The consultant feels as if he/she immediately, like a magician, has to 'pull a rabbit out of the hat'. There is, however, no hat, much less a rabbit to be had. What is to be done? The consultant needs to understand that the client is doing to the consultant what, in turn, is being done to the chief executive. On that basis, a degree of mutuality can be established and the pair – consultant and consultee – can embark on the process of working on what the underlying pressures/anxieties might be, and how to address them.

There are, of course, certain situations where a decision has to be made right there and then. This might be in the operating theatre of the emergency hospital, or in the plant room of a nuclear power station or the petroleum refinery at a moment of crisis. But these are rare exceptions. In most situations there is adequate time – as long as the pressure of flight into immediate action can be resisted and contained.

It is also tempting to make immediate decisions. It gives the impression of clear decisive leadership; it reassures the staff that the matter is in hand and something is being done; it reassures the leader that the matter has been dealt with. In a sense, it 'closes the book' of the decision-making process emotionally and organizationally speaking, so that all can get on with routine matters as before, 'untroubled' by the decision-making incident.

Decisions reached on this basis, however, have a distinct disadvantage. The first is that often the decision turns out to have been a 'pseudo-decision'. By this I mean a decision made unconsciously to rid oneself of the anxiety of not knowing what to do. It is a flight from the difficulty of living with the process of not knowing or powerlessness that often accompanies the early stages of decision-making. The pseudo-decision, therefore, masquerades as the real thing, whereas its actual purpose is to remove a degree of anxiety in the system, rather than to truly address the task at hand.

The second problem with a pseudo-decision, or for that matter of a well-thought-through-decision if poorly handled, is that, as I said, it 'closes the book' on the decision-making process. This means that a follow-up monitoring of the decision and its consequences is jettisoned.

It is clear that if decision-making is about the evaluation of different certainties and uncertainties in relation to the task of the organization, then any decision made can only be based on the present, here and now evidence as available, and has to be balanced and modified in the light of developments as the implementation of the decision occurs.

Monitoring, evaluating, and modifying are thus integral components of a true decision-making process, even as the implementation proceeds. A degree of 'porousness' in any decision is necessary in order for evidence-based modification. At worst, one must be open to the possibility that it was a poor, or ill-founded decision in the first place, and that consequences must, therefore, be faced. It must be recognized that mistakes are an integral part of decision-making, and acceptance of this fact is essential.

Any decision thus needs to be accompanied by a degree of alertness and light anxiety in monitoring its application within the system. A pseudo-decision, by contrast, can go into the emotional 'dealt with' outbox, and be closed until its unforeseen consequences cause it to dramatically re-surface in the 'for urgent action' box.

Andre Brink, the Nobel Prize winning author in his memoir *A Fork in the Road* (2009) quotes Yogi Berri as follows: 'when you come to a fork in the road take it'.

To the clearheaded conscious world business school trained chief executive this is 'wet nonsense'. Its strength, however, lies in the paradox it implies – taking one side of the fork does not mean that the presence of the other pathway should be ignored, even though taking the fork, as suggested, above might lead to some interesting unexpected consequences.

Chapter 13

The workforce and its make-up

There was a time when the social origin of the workforce and of middle and top management was fairly predictable. Nowadays, with the global economy and the spread of multinational workforces and global companies, the situation becomes more complex.

Of course, the mix of international cultures and assumptions needs to be taken into account when managing today's organizations. But in a more individual-specific way, the following scenario needs to be taken into account:

Example

An individual through good fortune, intelligence, and hard work rises beyond his/her social class stereotype and, as it were, becomes 'someone else' – 'no longer one of us'. This could be in terms of culture, social association, role, wealth, etc. The question then arises as to how this individual relates to his or her past and all that goes with it.

It may be that the individual is sympathetic to, and supportive of, others who come from a similar background with a similar pathway, and thus acts as a constructive role model for those attempting to follow in his or her footsteps.

In a multicultural international organization, such an individual would make a substantially positive 'integrative' contribution to the cultural mix and functioning of the organization.

It may, however, be that the individual cuts him or herself off from the past and all that it stands for, disowns his/her roots and culture, and, in the words of their original social group, becomes 'one of them'. This would have the opposite effect of the one described above, and would make for cultural differentiation, snobbism, and the denigration of certain classes and cultural elements in the company.

Example

Several recent histories of the Indian Raj clearly document that until just before independence there was hardly any social mixing, for example, in the Officer Classes of the Army. This served to keep the different elements apart – maintaining the social 'pecking order' but providing a poor role model for cooperation.

Similarly, the existence of different classes of eating or social facilities in public institutions or work organizations is divisive and anti-task. As one individual in an organizational consultancy put it, 'Those that get flowers in their offices, and those that don't'. Reward systems no doubt have their benefits but attention also needs to be given to the likely appearance of envy of those benefitting.

The dynamics described above are common, and in my experience never consciously maliciously intended. But they are 'noticed', particularly by those excluded from the 'perks' as perceived by them. It is not uncommon for individuals or groups of individuals to then have symbolic (if not real) filing cabinets full of grievances and wrongs that they have actually, or supposedly, been made to suffer. And 'when the time is ripe' depending on the institutional dynamics, and 'the last straw that broke the camel's back' dynamic has surfaced, the whole edifice comes crashing down, or at least is in serious trouble. As a management/leadership style and as a precaution, it is, therefore, far preferable to symbolically 'take off ones' shoes' and to put oneself into 'the others' shoes', at least some of the time: to consider how matters might look 'from the other side', and to consider whether a change needs to be made either in one's own behaviour or in institutional functioning.

Similarly, in sending a letter, an email, or a circular, it might be worthwhile giving thought to 'how might this be misinterpreted or misunderstood?' This, then, gives the opportunity to perhaps modify the message, retaining the original meaning, but reducing the risk of either everyday or wilful misunderstanding. As with a computer a 'spell check', a 'potential misunderstanding' check is advisable.

Chapter 14

The concept of the primary task of the organization

How is one to assess whether one's organization is effective or successful? Survival is one obvious criterion, but one that has to be seen in the context of the past, the future, and, more specifically, at what price to whom.

'Stakeholders' are individuals or structures that have an interest in the organization's success or lack thereof. Making a list of who the stakeholders of the organization are, or might be, is not that difficult. The problem arises when it comes to accommodating their various interests in the management and strategic vision of the organization. There is also the not uncomplicated matter of by what criteria success is to be measured.

Put another way, the question is: what is the primary task of the organization and who determines it? The primary task can also vary from time to time, and, for that matter, even from minute to minute. It also has to be understood that the primary task affects or determines how members conduct themselves, how they dress, and the language they use in their work. A middle-aged male in a pinstripe suit is unlikely to get on well with an adolescent on probation. Equally a woman dressed as a hippy is likely to have some problems in fitting in as a city banker.

The primary task is the task that has to be addressed at that particular moment, but it also must be seen in the context of the overall strategic direction of travel of the organization.

Example

A university professor in a medical school teaching hospital is conducting a seminar with a group of medical students. The primary task at that moment is teaching – an appropriate task given the setting.

The professor's emergency beeper goes off – there is a cardiac arrest in the casualty department, and he/she is the expert cardiologist on call. He/she rushes to the emergency department and embarks on resuscitating the patient with the cardiac arrest. The primary task has now become the resuscitation of the patient. Once the task has been completed the professor can turn to the group of students and resume teaching, preferably on the here and now experience of their having witnessed the resuscitation process. The primary task once again has become teaching. The task overall fits in with that of the hospital – to provide both teaching for students and medical services for patients.

If, instead of teaching, the professor had set up a poker school with the students, that activity could be described as anti-task – even given the present-day emphasis on hospitals as businesses. It would probably be somewhat far-fetched to say that playing poker with the students was in the service of developing good human relations between staff and students, and, therefore, increasing profitability.

However, even in the above hospital example there are conflicting pressures. How much time should the professor spend on teaching, how much on the provision of clinical services, and how much on research and publication? The dean of the medical school, the director of research, and the director of finance, and the chief executive of the whole outfit might all have widely contrasting views on where the emphasis should be. Unless all of the above-mentioned people have an awareness of the overall institutional 'soup' of ideals and tasks, the situation is likely to lead to undue stress and conflict.

Example

Take a simple example where being in touch with the primary task of the organization can make the difference between success and failure. A 'rave club' was running into difficulties. What is the primary task of a 'rave club'? Viewed unconsciously, its 'raves' are to provide excitement, delinquency, drugs, and sexual acting out. Not enough of the above brings failure; too much brings the attention of the police and possible shut-down. A careful balance of legitimate and illegitimate behaviour is thus required for survival. Similarly, what does a community dance club provide? It caters for the lonely in the community and is dependent on the provision of companionship for survival. If it does this it is successful, if not it is likely to fail.

Or take a manufacturing plant. Is its purpose to manufacture products, to create profit for the investors, provide employment for the local populace, or all of the above, including doing so in the most ecologically sound way possible?

Open cast mining would be a good symbol of achieving maximum production and profit returns, but also perhaps at maximum ecological cost. It would not be too far-fetched to think that in some organizations the management dynamic of the institution is an open cast mining attitude with little concern for the wellbeing of the staff and thus of the organization in the long term.

Given these dynamics, it is difficult to reach a sound enough balance when weighing up these pressures. It is also particularly difficult to find a neutral, thoughtful space in which the various conflicting pressures could be raised and decided on in an even-handed way. The problems obstructing the approach are two-fold. It is 'normal' human behaviour to play down and deny aspects of our own destructive behaviour, blaming others instead. 'Yes, it is true that there has been some river pollution from our factory, but that is nothing compared to what X factory over there does'.

As in a fractious marriage, it is always the partner who is the problem and who has to change, rather than acknowledging one's own contribution to the difficulties. The Old Testament talks about seeing 'the mote in your brother's eye and not the beam in your own'. Denial and projection into others (the other factory; one's partner) is thus one way of delaying any change in the service of more responsible production.

The second factor is that individual members of the management group or, for that matter, of the board, have different agendas to pursue – partly on account of their role, partly on the grounds of personality factors.

Example

The director of finance cannot lift his or her eyes out of the finance spreadsheets and also adopt the role, at least in part, of a 'responsible', 'in the round' member of the management group. He/she is doomed to suffer from finance spreadsheet tunnel vision. The chief operating officer focuses on production – the social and ecological consequences of which are someone else's problem. The human relations/personnel director is in essence there to placate the chief executive and to provide a sort of 'sin bin' for problematic members of staff. The chief executive is concerned about having a happy family atmosphere, even if this is achieved at the price of denial and repression of problems. Besides which, he/she has to worry about keeping the board onside, and about protecting his/her bonus.

The above might be perceived as an unduly cynical perspective, but once the irritation with this picture has passed, it is fair to say that there are elements of the above dynamic in all organizations. To summarize, it is a difficult task to stand one's ground, while at the same time having the freedom and generosity of mind to give your specific role up in order to discuss the situation from an overall, engaged, thoughtful-citizen state of mind. As previously mentioned, this is a so-called 'helicopter' or 'balcony' state of mind wherein one is observant yet adequately detached. It is essential that all involved at least attempt to do so.

Whether this can be achieved or not depends to a very large degree on the leader and leadership of the organization. The leader thus needs to be able, at times, to transcend the role of *pater* or *materfamilias* of a happy family and to make space for the tension, disorder, and argumentativeness that from time to time is the hallmark of a well-functioning family to be acknowledged and addressed.

With a variety of stakeholders it is unthinkable that a happy family dynamic could be the only norm. It could only occur if problems are repressed or denied – the result being that they are not publicly available to be addressed through common agreement and purpose.

Instead they are likely to 'leak out' into behind-the-scenes cabals, rumour, gossip, and sabotage. In all of the above instances the result is scheming, manipulation, and politicking that saps the morale, energy, and creativity that is needed to bring about solutions to everyday and future problems. It must be remembered that an organization cannot stand still. Developments in the social and industrial environment make for constant change, and this, of course, makes for an altered climate in which the organization needs to operate. The organizational organism thus needs to be in a constant 'adapt or fade away and die' type of state. To adapt is a matter of survival; it is not a matter of choice.

But what is adaptation? This dilemma returns us to the fundamentals of the primary task and its accompanying ideals. If there is no core ideal around which the adaptation takes place, then the risk is one of being so taken with the prevailing 'fashion', be it of production or of management, that the organization's success is threatened by its opportunistic stance. It thus becomes an organization that runs, in essence, on focus groups.

Each organization thus needs to give thought to what its core values are, and to what extent these need modifying as time progresses. Again, the core values can really only be related to if there is open discussion within the organization as to what these might be. This sort of debate is rarely embarked on, as members fear – sometimes rightly so – that a staggering difference of opinion will be revealed. They fear that instead of a degree of clarity about core values emerging, an atmosphere of distrust and enmity will arise that will only serve to make the situation worse.

The unspoken follow-up to this belief is a policy of 'let sleeping dogs lie'. This is understandable, and in line with the previously raised question of 'sweeping problems into the long grass', of delay and denial.

The problem with this is that 'sleeping dogs' always wake up at some time or another, usually choosing that time at their convenience – not ours. The result is problems arising when we are least prepared for them.

Difficult as it may seem, from time to time it is thus best to set aside a clearly bounded space, both in terms of geography and of time, for these matters to be addressed. As all 'insiders' from the chief executive down are also perceived to have 'fixed' views or blind spots, at times like this it can be useful to call upon the services of an independent outside consultant.

The task of the outside consultant would be to perform the role of a 'visiting anthropologist', i.e. to observe and comment on the behaviour of staff and the contents of their discussion (see Part 5 for more on consultation). The consultant also encourages participants to make links between their views as expressed and these observations. This to be done against a perspective of the stated task of the meeting. If the task of the meeting, for example, is to review the core values of the organization, then it would obviously be helpful to look at these against the perspective of the future. Issues of who, in what role, and by when, are to be discussed. The realization that this should be embarked on is obviously a problem emotionally. Sadly, the result is often one of 'Thank you for your help – we are now aware of the picture and will proceed with this ourselves'. This result means that – problems are again being kicked into the long grass. In part, this can be dealt with by follow-up meetings with the consultant.

Chapter 15

On the innate dynamics of groups

The first question that needs to be addressed is: is there, in fact, such a thing as a group dynamic? Are eight people sitting around the boardroom table to manage the organization a management group with a group-dynamic interplay, or are they just eight individuals who happen to be in a meeting. Of course, they are eight separate individuals who bring to the meeting their formal tasks and roles; however, they also bring issues of gender, age, race, and experience, both professional and personal. And, as already mentioned, they bring their unconscious experiences of life in the form of the 'emotional lenses' through which they see the world.

Take eight separate individuals in a room relating to each other on a common task, for example, an agenda item on the future of the company. Where do group processes come into the matter?

The opinion of professionals in the field of human relations is that a group is more than a collection of individuals, and that, apart from the individual processes mentioned above, there is such a phenomenon as a group process.

One might even question what 'an individual' actually is. The moment a baby is born it is part of a group, and the very process of the family and friends seeing the newborn triggers a multitude of assumptions and opinions about it that will, in part, consciously and unconsciously determine its future. Some of this can be captured in the process of naming the child, where along with the name comes a series of assumptions about the baby's future behaviour.

Example

'He looks just like uncle Jake – let's call him Jake'. (Uncle Jake being the black sheep of the family.)

Take an example at the other extreme. Is it possible to be a hermit without there being a group? Is the hermit not that member of the group who rejects the group process and adopts the hermit group process. A hermit without a group is not a hermit, he/she is a singleton. Again let us look at, say, the state of mind of a lynch mob or of the Nuremberg Rallies. Of course, there are differences in size between the above and the calm of an eight-member management group. But can one really deny that in the above-mentioned two examples we are really talking about only a collection of people, or is there something else – in this instance, a large group process is at play.

The implication of the presence in the meeting of a group process is that, apart from the conscious concrete roles that people perform, there are also other processes at work that, if unchecked, can interfere with the decision-making processes and the task of the meeting. The risk of unconscious group dynamics interfering with the task of the meeting is greater if the meeting is not managed in what one might call work-mode, and instead is left to run its course in a *laissez-faire* sort of way.

When you are a member or manager/leader of a group, it is essential that there is a focus on viewing and thinking about the unconscious group processes at play. We are all clear about the conscious roles/reasons why members are present and participate in a management group meeting. If the meeting is well managed as regards task, boundaries, and time, chances are that there will only be minimal interference in its work by the presence of unconscious processes. The more the meeting runs in a *laissez-faire* or sloppy mode, the more are unconscious processes likely to make their appearance and interfere with the required work.

As mentioned, each member of the group also has an unconscious role to play in the group. Thus, in a loose group, as described above, members behave along the lines of their previously developed roles and functions and are likely to conduct themselves according to these criteria: the supportive one, irrespective of facts, the unreliable one, the fainthearted one, the martyr, the macho one, etc. Most irritating are the 'pain in the backside' members who are often disowned by the 'goodies' in the group. The natural response is to see it as the personal problem of the individual concerned (let's call him Fred again), and to occupy themselves with thoughts about how to get rid of him. At times this is necessary, but it is more common for the 'unconscious vacancy' to then be filled by a newcomer who performs exactly the same unconscious role as the member who was fired. A more productive way of dealing with the problem is to consider that the offending member is, in fact, drawing attention to a taboo or denied subject that is disowned by the remaining members of the group. The 'pit canary', drawing attention to the 'negative psychic fumes' in the meeting/organization, is thus performing a vital role towards a sober functioning of the discussion, the meeting, and the institution. It is a little far-fetched to propose that the chair says, 'Thank you, Fred, for raising this difficult perspective. I think that to a degree you are speaking for a part of all of us, so let us spend some time on the issues you raised'. Such a response would be a healthy way of dealing with so-called win–win situations which are essentially built on a denial of the complexity of the issues involved. Thinking about what the unconscious roles are of the individual members of a group, and also thinking about one's own valency, one's own tendency to fall into unconscious group roles, is an essential part of competent personal and institutional functioning. Viewed this way, Fred is thus acknowledged to be bringing useful elements for discussion, and in doing so also partly relieves himself of being stuck in that onerous role. He also helps others to present a more rounded response to matters being discussed. It also saves money and HR time!

There is another important element that needs to be taken account of in thinking about groups: specific dynamics related to the size of the group, whatever its task. A two-some group is the cornerstone of good working relationships. Perhaps in this configuration it is easy to see how poor or inadequate experience in earlier life can be unconsciously re-enacted in later adult personal and work life, and be a handicap. When it comes to a three-some group the dynamic changes particularly if they are of equal status, e.g. production manager, sales manager, and director of finance. In such a configuration, the dynamic is often one of a pair and the third 'left out'. If the one who is left out 'rotates' as it were, then the situation is manageable, but if two are constantly 'ganging up' on the one then basic primitive processes can be evolved that are highly problematic. This could lead to decisions being taken not on the basis of sound conscious work-related principles, but on the basis of hurt and retaliation. Moreover, the situation can be exacerbated if the work element of the meeting is mishandled, thus leaving space for personal issues to surface. Who is 'in' and who is 'out' will rotate in some sort of conscious or unconscious way, but the essential dynamic of a three-some will always be present and influence the group's capacity to work.

Groups of four, five, or six often unconsciously recreate aspects of family dynamics, and although they have the capacity to work well, the unconscious echoes of family 'pecking order' dynamics are often not far away. Groups of eight to ten are the ideal work sized groups and if handled with an eye to the task in hand can achieve a great deal.

Once you get over the size of 15 or so it becomes increasingly difficult to hold the entire group simultaneously in your mind, and to encompass what each member stands for. In such groups work can really only be carried out in sub-groups that operate separately from the group of 15. The latter then serves the function of agreeing or not what has been decided outside.

Once we get into largish 25 or more or large groups of 50 plus there is the risk of losing one's personal identity and becoming a group particle – witness in very extreme examples lynch mobs or the Nuremberg rallies. Turquet describes this as 'identity as per the skin of my neighbour'. The chances of such dynamics occurring, for example, in a work meeting of all employees, are obviously lessened if the task of the meeting is clearly stated, and the meeting is managed both concretely and psychologically to perform a clearly related work task.

In conclusion, it needs to be noted that there are certain given dynamics innately related to the size of the group and in setting up a group, or being a member of or managing or leading such a group, these dynamics will always be there and have an effect on the functioning of the group.

Chapter 16

On leadership and followership

If we look at leadership from the perspective of human development, and at where we might first come across the roots of leadership, then it is perhaps logical to start with early mother–child relationships. While it could be said that that is too far-fetched to have any relevance to the topic, if one thinks of such expressions as the 'mother or the father of the nation', for example, or 'like father like son' or 'the apple does not fall far from the tree' there are parallel, if unconscious, assumptions in that statement.

So what does a mother or the person performing a mothering relationship (who may be a mother substitute, a carer, a father, an older sibling) actually do for the baby? They do their best to look after the baby's needs. Initially this will take the form of taking care of the baby's bodily needs, but in doing so they will also be setting the emotional structures of the baby's inner world. Starting from the child's genetic make-up and building on that (some people would add the child's intra-uterine and birth experience), it begins to develop an image of the world and its place in it. It will also begin to have an experience, not necessarily conscious or verbal, of what its care is like. Are its needs being met or not? Is there a reliable carer out there that one can trust? Or is one left to get on with things as best one can, without the reassurance of an outside presence? We are talking about a more-or-less wholly dependent state of mind. This is not the sort of state one would wish for in an adult relationship, or more specifically in a work relationship, but nevertheless one that, at times, occurs in adult life.

But recent research on the early child–carer relationship has shown that even in the very first phase the child's response to the mother also has an effect on the latter – so even there, it is a case of a two-way relationship, despite not being one of equal partners.

Could one say that there is a 'leadership' component in this early relationship? I believe so in as much as the mother provides the setting for the child's development, but the child, too, makes a contribution to the question of what its needs are and when they are to be met. This process of intervention might be at times, if not often, frustrating to the parents, but is perhaps not that different from the tension between the leadership and followership in an organization.

As the child develops it begins to acquire skills that, in turn, make for growth and independence, for example, wanting to feed itself, toilet training, etc. All need to be encouraged, but also managed and contained by the carer.

We then get into the 'terrible twos' (or threes) when matters of power and authority need to be negotiated; whose will shall prevail, and through what process? Will the child's wishes be crushed by disciplinary force, only to re-emerge in a hormonally turbo-charged way in adolescence? Will there be a process of dialogue and negotiation in which both parties participate? (Possibly the early roots of the so-called 'win–win' business negotiation philosophy).

As the child develops it becomes clear that it has to learn about its power and authority, or lack thereof, and to learn these matters in relation to its world. In the course of its growth and development it also begins to meet a succession of others with whom the same issues need to be negotiated – father, siblings, and other family members; later on the peer group in kindergarten or its equivalent, teachers of various sorts, authority figures of various kinds, both academic and societal.

So when the individual reaches the stage of employment, of working with colleagues in a joint enterprise, he or she comes with a wealth of experience of how matters of relatedness and relationships might be managed, or for that matter mismanaged.

The idea that management or leadership skills might be taught as part of an in-house training course or an MBA at a prestigious business school thus needs to be seen in perspective. Whatever is being taught, and however useful it is, must be seen as something that is, in effect, 'grafted', in the horticultural sense, onto the 'rootstock' of the individual's previous experience. In horticulture the rootstock determines various elements of the overall plant – in essence the vigour, height, and fruitfulness of the end product.

As in horticulture, some grafts take exceptionally well and the rootstock and grafted-on material are compatible. In other instances, the two are incompatible or problematic and require a third component of plant material between rootstock and graft. This intermediate element could be seen as the symbolic equivalent of coaching, counselling, or therapy.

Example

A situation in which in the 360-degree feedback of a top executive the universal message is that 'he doesn't listen', it is not enough for that person to leave the event with the resolution that 'I must work harder at listening'. If you don't and can't listen, telling yourself to listen more or better is not likely to have a very lasting effect. For a start, you will, in all likelihood, respond to the feedback itself by 'not listening'. This often takes the form of falling into a defensive state of 'Ah yes, I know who put that into the feedback', or 'It's a cultural difference', etc. Both of the above might be true, but neither will improve the situation.

The fundamental question is: 'why does that person not listen?', or 'what in his/her development has led to this particular state of mind and its related problems?' It is only when you have some idea of what the *cause* of the problem is that you can begin to address it. This applies whether it is an engineering problem that is to be addressed, or a psychological one.

The basic psychological idea is that our adult behaviour is the result of years of apprenticeship and learning in the school of personal growth and development. As we enter the years of productive adult life, whether in the personal or work arena, we bring with us a whole series of assumptions, many conscious and a great many unconscious, as to how we conduct ourselves, both in relation to the tasks in hand and to others.

As regards managing ourselves and others, we will have had experience of leadership and of followership, as well as of wrestling with the odd mixture of the two on a regular basis.

In line with the idea that the soundest form of adult behaviour – in this case in the area of leadership – is based on respecting the learning of the past, it is essential that in any adult professional role, whether as member, follower or leader, one should remain in touch with the other role components of one's personal and professional life, even though perhaps they are not being exercised at the present time. Thus the story of the Sultan of Baghdad who disguised himself in ordinary clothes and wandered the streets and markets of his kingdom at night to hear what his subjects had to say. The capacity from time to time to step into followership shoes, both concretely and symbolically, is an important element of leadership.

Equally, if followers never have the opportunity to step into leadership roles, for example, in 'acting up' at times, or having challenging tasks delegated to them, their development is likely to be held back or stunted with negative effects on the organization's effectiveness as such.

So what is the role of 'leader'? Starting from basics, it is to provide a setting in which the work of the primary task of the organization can be carried out responsibly. This, amongst other tasks, means that, to a degree, the leader has to shield the workforce from undue anxiety about the pressures of the outside world. I stress the word undue. Not being in touch with the pressures of the outside world, whether the outside world refers to the world of the competitive industry they are in, or global society at large, means that they are out of touch with the reality of external processes and change. A manufacturer who is not in touch with technical and social developments in the outside world is on the path to bankruptcy. On the other hand, the importation of 'breathless anxiety' of developments elsewhere in the industry or in the world is equally bound to be problematic. Staff being swamped in, and overwhelmed by, imported anxieties cannot get on with their work, again, to the detriment of the functioning of their organization.

The task of the leader is thus to feedback appropriate amounts of external world reality to those inside, enough for them to be in touch with developments, but not so much as to be overwhelmed.

Equally important is the leader's capacity to feed to the outside world what is going on in the organization/institution that he/she represents, and making sure that the external representation thereof also takes cognisance of the societal contribution made.

The leader thus needs to, as it were, be positioned on the boundary, rather like the two-headed dog Cerberus of ancient Greek mythology who looked two ways, both inward and outward. In biological terms, the leader needs to function as a semi-osmotic membrane, managing and monitoring the information from outside in and inside out.

This could be called the containing function of leadership, meaning, to a degree, that the leader has to 'leach out' inappropriate or toxic concentrations of anxiety or uncertainty in the system. In that regard, the leader functions as the 'kidney' in a bodily system that needs to have a way of eliminating the waste products arising from both the emotional and industrial processes in the organization.

How does one get to be a leader? Organizationally one gets appointed and given the authority to lead by the responsible organization. Thus, we the board of X having the authority from a role in the organization appoint you as leader. Authority to lead has, however, two roots. One is listed above; the other is the candidate's internal conviction that they have what it takes to perform in the role. To be effective, the leader needs both.

Should there be elements of doubt in the system about the capacity to lead then organization problems are likely to occur. Ambivalent appointments are often accompanied by a lack of resources so that the capacity to be an effective leader is undermined. A fuller way of showing ambivalence is by making the required appointment but making sure that someone is appointed who is known to be ineffective or incompetent.

The leader needs to pay serious attention to the primary task of the organization and that decisions are made in the service of that task.

There needs to be clarity about being authoritative as opposed to authoritarian. Authoritative means that decisions are made in the service of the direction of travel of the primary task. Authoritarian instead describes a style of leadership that brooks no questioning or discussion of decisions and primarily serves the narcissistic personal aspects of the leader.

Leadership by definition must have a clear team commutative component.

In the present climate of open electronic information, the days of leadership by diktat are over and the way ahead must include the team component.

Bullying is an activity that has become more of an issue in running an organization. Decisions made in line with the primary task of the organization are often resisted and called bullying.

If the decision made is clearly in line with the task of the organization, and stated to be so, it could be called 'task orientated' but not 'bullying'. Anti-task behaviour needs to be recognized as such and dealt with. It needs to be understood that in any intended change, even if supposedly welcomed, there will be resistance; and time, patience, and discussion need to be allowed for it to be implemented.

A key element for the survival of any organization is the bringing in of new talent from outside, taking into account the likely ambivalent response to such a process as outlined previously, but also to bring on ideas and individuals from within. Training and development programmes are important here, but in my view by far the most important, but also by far the most effective and difficult growth programme involves in-house delegation. Delegation is often seen as a way of unburdening senior staff from relatively menial tasks in order for them to have more time to focus on matters of importance. While that may be a good enough reason, it is not uncommon for senior staff to cling to menial 'housekeeping' tasks and micromanage issues as a way of avoiding tackling the much more stressful 'important tasks' regarding the strategic future of the organization.

There is, however, another and vastly more important reason for delegation and this is in order to bring on existing staff, creating a developmental flow, and making it clear that senior staff are not indispensable and are expected to move on at some point.

Resistance to the process of delegation takes two forms. Those who should delegate are resistant for reasons to be discussed, while those who should take on being delegated to can be equally resistant. There is thus an axis of resistance involving both sides of the equation. It is, therefore, not surprising that, as a result, there is often little movement or change in the delegation arena.

Those who need to delegate believe that if they do what needs doing themselves, it will be done more clearly, more to task, more reliably, and with less of a chance of complications. They regard those to whom the tasks are to be delegated as slower, less competent, more likely to miss deadlines, and more likely to create problems which will then be attributed to the person having done the delegation in the first place. The person being delegated to, in turn, is likely to fall into a state of anxiety of not being able to 'do the job' and to stand revealed and exposed in their inexperience and incompetence. They also run the risk of being attacked by their peer-group rivals.

There is some degree of truth in both perspectives, but in only having this perspective several points important to the wellbeing of the organization and its future are missed. First, there is the point made above of there being a responsibility, for both the good of the organization, and its staff, for there to be a 'developmental stream'.

Second, we need to remind ourselves that an essential part of learning is making mistakes and learning from them. If the climate is one in which it is made absolutely sure that no mistakes could possibly happen, it would be a climate of anxiety, persecution, and one with neither innovation nor creativity. Mistakes would still happen as is inevitable, but they would be 'buried' with the result that no 'learning from mistakes' could or would take place.

Third, there is an unspoken but not uncommon further issue, particularly for those that delegate, which occurs when the person delegated to not only performs the task well, but does so in a way that is more innovative, and also possibly more effective, than had been foreseen by the delegator. If the latter person is of a generous and supportive disposition he/she would obviously recognize the talent and support it. More common is a response of feeling overtaken and 'shown up' for one's age and rigidity by a younger person, with the inevitable consequence of wishing to see the individual as 'too big for their boots' and needing to be 'taken down a peg or two'. The unconscious dynamic is the projection of competence upwards and the projection of incompetence downwards. Both are false, but ensure pseudo-stability in the system.

As mentioned before, while new ideas and creativity in organizations have much lip service paid to them, the reality is that both people and organizations feel more comfortable with their existing ideas than with having to consider, accommodate and implement new ones.

Apart from the dynamic of the leader providing a containing setting conducive to personal and institutional growth, there is still the need for a vision for the future of the organization.

Looking to the future

In my view, managers mostly, in essence, manage the status quo. Leaders, by contrast, must focus on the future – and must, therefore, have a vision of how things might be in years to come. It is captured by the oft-quoted image of Martin Luther King Jr's 'I have a dream ...'. Such a dream or vision for the future must be based on an awareness of present-day reality, but at the same time must make allowance for a degree of structured unreality and hoped-for wish-fulfilment.

An essential component of this is the capacity to look ahead without being 'spooked' by the uncertainty that this entails.

A leader must thus have the capacity to consider a long time-horizon for self, but much more importantly for the organization itself. This is a difficult thing to achieve, because the longer the time-horizon, and the farther the goal, the more uncertainty there is. Uncertainty in the decision-making, and thus leadership, process is a seedbed for anxiety. The further one looks ahead the more uncertainty, the more anxiety, and thus the more likely the avoidance of the leadership task.

It is, therefore, no wonder that leaders unconsciously allow themselves to be 'swallowed up' by distractions. Emails, crises, 'household' and management tasks, micromanagement – anything is better than having time and space for thought to consider the future.

The same can be said for routine, which makes for a comfortable state of knowing exactly where you stand and what is to be done. In some situations and organizations routine is essential for the safe well-functioning of a system, for example, in a surgical operating theatre where every instrument used is counted in and out, and everyone knows their role and what is expected of them. It can equally be said that in other situations routines are mindless, bureaucratic processes to ensure that no innovation or change creeps into the system.

When it comes to leadership, many different styles have been described, and many psychological and other devices constructed to measure and categorize leadership style. There are a great many systems for describing and categorizing leadership styles, but one often wonders: 'so what do I do with this categorisation of myself, and how do I implement this understanding constructively?' So one comes across leaders who describe themselves as a 'so and so system of evaluation' person. So what! What is to be done about that?

Whatever the style, it seems to me that there are several key essential features of leadership that need to be addressed: the first is the nature of the relationship between leadership and followership in the organization. The second, and related, issue is the question of what price is exacted for the particular style of leadership in operation. Taking followership first, there is a spectrum to be considered. On the one hand there might be an expectation of abject, dependent followership in which all thought, wisdom, and leadership is seen to be held in the leader. What is expected of the followers is mindless and often adoring compliance along the lines of 'without him we are lost'.

Example

One of the best examples of this occurs in the Apocrypha, in which there is a lengthy description of the preparation that Holofernes, Nebuchadnezzar's general, makes in his campaign against the Israelites. Holofernes obviously had a marvellous public relations apparatus, and everything to do with the magnificence of the campaign referred back to him.

When in his sleep he had his head chopped off by Judith, his lover, and she displayed it to his troops from the walls of the Israeli fortifications, they, as Freud originally described it, literally 'lost their head' and fled in disorder. Here is an example where undue dependence on one head with no alternative adequate forms of leadership meant disaster for the followership.

Example

Apart from the everyday examples of totalitarian leadership available to us in daily news channels, the case of Jim Jones the cult leader of a sect in Guyana makes the point. He ordered his followers to 'drink the Kool-Aid' even though it later became known that they knew it had been poisoned, yet they drank it all and died.

At the other end of the leadership/followership spectrum is the leader who encourages ideas, challenges, and leadership elements in the *followers*, and who at times is prepared to assume a followership role under the leadership of a follower. This makes for a situation in which the maximum possible creativity of the group can be harnessed in the service of the task.

Importantly, this is to be distinguished from abrogated, indecisive, or incompetent leadership in which clarity and decisions are avoided, with resultant chaos.

Apart from a concern about leadership and followership, a leader must also have the capacity to observe and deal with the dynamics of group processes, on the board, in the management committee of the organization, and in the organization overall.

It is not uncommon for conditions to exist in leadership structures in which it is unclear as to who is responsible for what particular functions and tasks, and where the boundaries between different roles and departments are unclear. This situation is often tolerated, one might even say at times unconsciously welcomed, because it shields individuals from responsibility and blame should something go wrong, or should something need to be done. The individuals concerned can thus rest comfortably in their positions, as the question of what is to be done – and who is to be blamed – can be put on someone else's shoulders – a process that has the equivalent dynamic of the children's game of 'pass the parcel', except that, in this instance, unlike in the children's game, no one wants to have the contents of the parcel.

On the surface an organization that functions like this gives the impression that it is well-run and on top of things. It is, therefore, difficult for a newcomer to ask 'dumb-seeming' questions about 'who does what', and 'what are my particular tasks and responsibilities'. In fact, it is not uncommon for there to be either no job description or no updated job description, or for that matter a discussion, both with the newly appointed individual or with the group of colleagues in management, about what the specific tasks and roles are.

It is yet another case of 'let sleeping dogs lie' – the real problem only comes to light when there is a crisis of one sort or another, and there is then no mechanisms for dealing with the problem in the context of cooperation by all. Instead, and not surprisingly, it triggers a dynamic of blame and dissent, which only makes the problem worse.

Followership is at least as important as leadership. Ignoring the followership element, and/or taking it for granted is a common mistake. Followership may be seen as the equivalent of driving on the motorway in an under-powered car and tucking into the slipstream of a large fast-moving truck ahead. It works in the short term but has clear risks to all involved in the longer term. Followership is thus treated as a passive group staff process instead of being an active contribution to the momentum of the institution. Not only does it carry the severe risk of disaster, as illustrated in the Holofernes example, but it also underestimates and undervalues the individual and group contributions that make for an innovative and creative organization.

As often happens, the latter individuals are likely to feel undervalued and as a result take their initiatives and ideas elsewhere, depriving the 'mother organisation' of the creative green shoots of production, or of producing new products and services.

The leadership/followership dynamic is also directly related to the matter of delegation, in which a reversal of roles from time to time is required. The follower sometimes must 'step-up' and take on more of a leadership role, and the leader needs to step down for a while to let the 'delegate' get on with it. In this scenario, there is learning to be done by both parties concerned once they have overcome the anxiety of the required changes in role. There is also a good deal of useful learning to be had in looking at the institutional functioning when the leader is away. Who has stepped into the breach, who has ducked out of the responsibility, etc.? It is a case of professionally taking off one's traditional roles/shoes and trying on another pair.

For the institution, it is an essential part of the process of bringing on the next generation while ensuring a good supply of candidates for upcoming roles and development.

Chapter 17

Risks inherent in the leadership role

At some level we all overtly or covertly have a desire to be a leader, even perhaps those who fervently proclaim that the last thing on earth they want is a leadership role, and that blessed followership is their true ambition in life. One can see the early negotiations about leadership, the joys and pitfalls of the process, if one takes the time to observe what children get up to in playtime at their kindergarten or primary school: 'my gang', 'your gang', best friends, enemies, etc. Leadership at this early stage is about popularity or the lack thereof, and how, if possible, to keep one's position in the melee, whether as leader elsewhere in the specific pecking order.

These early behaviours, with their accompanying triumphs or set-backs, to some extent set the pattern of behaviour in later group and institutional settings, as one embarks on one's life pattern in social and work environments.

Once one achieves the position of, say, chief executive, or president, or chair, or head of department, or of group, the same issues remain in place. One wants to be loved and valued. At the same time one perhaps recognizes that, if one is to perform one's role well, one cannot base it on being loved.

The primary task one has to perform is to act in the service of one's organizational role. This might very well necessitate making decisions that cause one *not* to be loved – possibly even to be hated. To manage on the basis of being loved would thus be based on anti-task behaviour in one's role. The risk to one in a leadership role is thus, as described above, to base one's conduct on the wish to elicit love from those one leads. One way of achieving this is to leave the 'unlovely' (if one might call them that) decisions to someone else. We might see a parallel with the 'loving mother' who says to the transgressing child, 'You just wait till your father comes home'.

Or on a ship, there may be a dynamic in which the captain is loved and the first officer is hated. This dynamic is perhaps quite comfortable for the captain, and at times possibly even for the first officer, if he/she is that way personally inclined. However, it requires ducking the responsibilities of one's actions for the captain to behave as if he/she didn't have a firm side, and for the first officer to deny his/her caring side. In the family example: the mother behaves as if she didn't have an authoritative and disciplining side, and father's caring and loving side is not given a chance to reveal itself.

There is a constant risk of being derailed from performing the task one has, by being diverted onto a track of being loved or being feared and hated. An awareness of this risk, and standing out against it, does not, of course, mean that one should not consider the consequences of one's actions and plough on regardless. The equation thus arises of what needs to be done in one's role, and considering the repercussions it will have on the employees, the community, etc.

A risk of a different sort arises from 'hardening' oneself against the consequences of one's actions – developing 'a thick skin' and not bothering to examine the outcome of one's actions. This state of mind might even be presented as forceful or decisive. It might well be both, but could also be described as blundering, bullying and insensitive.

The dynamics I have described above do not only affect the leader in his/her professional role, his/her position as role model, and, therefore, the atmosphere in the whole organization. It also has an effect on the personal life of the leader. Being a tyrannical, micromanaging leader at work is unlikely to lead to a 'pussycat' style of behaviour at home, which is unlikely to be conducive to harmonious family dynamics.

Example

A member of a review group got 360-degree feedback from her work colleagues that she should be more direct and authoritative. This didn't seem too difficult a task to achieve as she had shown such a side to her behaviour on her business school programme. Following that programme she reported equivalent progress at work. When followed up she said, 'mind you – my husband recently said to me "darling I'm not one of your direct reports"!' All behaviour needs to be seen in the perspective of setting and context.

Part 3

Self and workplace dynamics

Chapter 18

The use of self in one's work life

It used to be thought that the most professional and correct way of going about one's work role was to leave both one's personal life outside, and to enter work free of emotion or feeling. This state of mind is often also concretely enacted by the use of a prescribed form of dress for the specific role. Thus the bewigged and gowned judge handing down a death sentence is communicating, 'I am not here as a person with a vendetta against you – I am here in role as a judge performing a role required of me by the state and by society'. Death sentences are now, by and large, abolished, but sentences that have a serious effect on individuals' lives and families are still a regular occurrence.

The same is true of a nurse's uniform which proclaims 'I am not here as an ordinary person relating to you – I am here as a nurse and it is thus acceptable for me to see you, a stranger, naked'. However, even when you are protected or shielded from everyday human interaction by your role-specific dress or setting, you are still subject to feelings, emotions, and thoughts as you go about your work. What, if anything, can be done about this? It used to be thought that the best way of approaching these feelings is to 'put such thoughts out of your mind' – ignore them, repress them, deny them.

A certain quantum of the above mechanism is, indeed, necessary for one to securely stay in the role. At the same time, personal responses persist. If the thoughts are personal, then not much can be done, apart from being careful that personal feelings do not intrude into, and interfere with, one's work role and conduct. Nevertheless, there is a different angle from which we can view the matter. What if the feelings that one experiences are not solely one's own, but signals from the environment that one is picking up?

Initially, such a thought seems utterly far-fetched and fanciful. Surely our own feelings are, as we have always assumed, our own feelings, and that's the end of it. Or not? This is true to an extent. However, perhaps the matter is somewhat more complicated than would appear. What if we picked up subliminal or even unconscious signals from the environment, experienced them, and then interpreted – or miss-interpreted – them as our own. Such subliminal signals might be in the shape of smell or sound or peripheral vision – all faculties we possess that are known to be essential building blocks of development in infant growth. Therefore, we now have the possibility that the feelings and thoughts that we experience have a *twofold* input. One from within ourselves, consisting of our past and also our present 'here and now' feelings, and one from the external stimuli mentioned above. Our experiences are based on an interplay of the two.

Pursuing this matter further, i.e. questioning whether one's 'stream' at each moment is predominantly internal or external, would not be hugely worthwhile were it not for the fact that emotions and thoughts arising in the individual may bring crucial elements of understanding to what is 'really' going on.

A metaphor for this might be an electric circuit into which a measuring instrument is linked, giving a reading of the activity of the circuit. Entering an organization as an outsider – a consultant, for example – could be seen to perform the same function as the measuring device. One would have to enter the organization as an 'instrument', having 'cleared' oneself by thinking about how and what one is feeling. The instrument is in the 'on' position, with a neutral reading phase. Next, one observes how one feels and thinks as contact with the organization proceeds.

The hypothesis is that the reading one gets in observing one's thoughts and feelings *may* have something to do with what is going on in the organization. One may possibly take enough of a reading to form a hypothesis about the workings of the organization, without enough hard evidence to be certain. Along with other theories and sources, a tentative hypothesis of this kind might be worth pursuing.

The assumption in this approach is that one allows oneself, free of preconception, to be immersed in the 'unconscious soup' – the institutional unconscious – of the organization, and to see what, if anything, rises to the surface of one's mind.

This could be seen as the emotional equivalent of using and valuing peripheral vision instead of pursuing the 'tunnel vision' of preconception.

The above approach is by no means a substitute for everyday conscious, active business-related approaches to management, leadership, or coaching, but at times it can be a valuable source of the 'hunch' that begins the process, hopefully leading to a breakthrough in understanding down the line.

The whole matter is well illustrated by the following apocryphal story:

> a man is taking his dog for a walk at night. He comes across a man searching the pavement under a streetlight. The dog-walker enquires, 'what are you doing?' The man replies, 'I am looking for my car keys that I have lost'. The dog-walker enquires, 'have you lost them here?' The man replies, 'no, but the light is better here'.

The story highlights the practice of how often we revert to dealing with problems along our usual orthodox lines that, at some level, we know don't work, and how reluctant we are to attempt to find answers where 'the light is not so good'. The above-mentioned technique of using *ourselves* as an instrument to pick up institutional dynamics might be an example of applying aspects of the latter approach.

Example

A speaker was invited to give a post-dinner speech for the senior staff of a bank. In introducing the speaker the bank's president announced that that very afternoon a merger had been agreed between their bank and a rival bank. The news was presented as being excellent – 'a win–win situation' for all – and a great future was to be expected for the new conjoined organization. The president then sat down and handed the podium to the after-dinner speaker. The meeting at that point felt completely flat and the speaker became more and more distracted and depressed. Finally, on reflection, he stopped and said, 'I think we cannot proceed with the planned speech as the president's announcement has completely shifted the ground on which we have been based'. What followed was a lively discussion on the positives of the change, but also on the negatives and fears! 'Would we have to reapply for our jobs?' 'Would there be redundancies and where?' etc. The speaker's change of mode was based, essentially, on his own feeling in himself. After-dinner speakers are, after all, used to what is called the 'graveyard slot dynamic' but this event was different, as evidenced by the lively discussion that followed once the topic had been changed. Initially, the president was upset at the change of tack – he had somehow hoped to 'slip in' the announcement with no further discussion at the event, or possibly ever. With time he was, however, appreciative of the wider discussion which eventually led to a sound enough piece of work in merging the two organizations.

Example

Following a public lecture on change and resistance to change, the speaker is invited to consult for a religious organization who had become stuck when tasked with the role of updating the functioning of the order, its use of its substantial resources, and its role in society. The consultant meets with the committee and, despite the committee's competence and the consultant's positive attitude and years of experience, the consultant falls more and more into a paralyzed and stuck state of mind, just like the committee.

Before the next meeting some weeks later, it is announced that the venue of the meeting needs to be changed. The consultant is then led through a labyrinth of rooms to the new venue where the meeting is to take place. The guide comments on the premises they walk through: 'this is the private chapel of the Princess X'. 'This altarpiece was done by Bramante'. 'This ceiling was painted by Michelangelo', and so on. A 'light' went on in the mind of the consultant. He realized that they had all been stuck on account of the glory and presence of the ancestors and felt insignificant, small, and impotent in the light of the latter's achievements. Once this suggestion was raised, the emotional log jam shifted and impressive progress was made in adapting the use of the premises to meet present-day needs. It was the consultant's feelings, as he concretely and symbolically traversed the past, that gave the vital clue as to what was paralyzing the work of the present committee.

Helpful as these thoughts might be, the tentative, uncertain, and provisional nature of any material or understanding arising from one's personal feeling must be acknowledged. Any hypothesis arising from the above approach ought to be prefaced with introductions such as 'could it possibly be that?' or 'have you ever considered?' or 'might there be such a phenomenon as X at play?' It is surprising how often such an enquiry opens up another pathway of understanding. One must also be prepared for the answer to the above pattern of hypothesis to be 'no', in which case one is to some extent back to square one.

But any hypothesis, however tentative, must be framed against the backcloth of the primary task of the organization, and any hypothesis must preferably be backed by a limited degree of evidence. Hence: 'I've observed that ... could it possibly be that it points in the following direction?'

Warning! Anything more specific than that might well be correct, but the price of such certainty is likely to be the fostering of a degree of omnipotence and hubris in the leader/consultant/coach, thus creating a degree of dependency in the client that is likely to obstruct the teamwork of the organization.

Chapter 19

On listening

In listening to what is being said, both at a conscious level and in the unconscious subtitles, taking into account one's own feelings and emotions, it is equally important to consider what is *not* being said.

If someone describes how their early life led on to their present work position with no mention of parents, family, siblings, or community, then it may be a matter of interest. Perhaps they are alerting one to an important closed 'enclave'. It may be that there is nothing much of relevance in this particular area, but, on the other hand, it could say something about the individual's relatedness to his environment and the world. This, in turn, might be a dynamic that is unconsciously replayed in the work setting with predictable results. If you're a singleton or a 'self-made man' who does not feel the need for others, there may be certain advantages in that, and it may lead to a certain type of success. However, it may also have associated problems in your work and personal life.

Over time, individuals develop defensive veneers that keep people at bay and act as a shield against what is seen as intrusive probing. We all need elements of defensiveness, but these defensive shields can also imprison us in thoughts and actions that are detrimental to us and our relationships. Relationships are, after all, to a large extent, based on mutually agreed elements of interpersonal probing.

The style of listening is also worth looking at. One way of avoiding hearing what is said and its implications is to listen to 'the other side' only to pick holes in their argument in order to be able to retaliate and shoot them down. The opposing view is thus ignored and only used as material for a counter-attack. This is a long way from listening with an 'open mind' which allows for the recognition that one's opponent has a legitimate view. Also that it is legitimate to look at and assess the validity of one's own view.

What is also painfully visible particularly in political negotiations/ settlements is that a supposed agreed form of words, in fact, has directly opposite meanings to the antagonists. It thus takes the form of being a face-saving type of window dressing behind which the issues remain unresolved and thus not in a position to be worked at in a more satisfactory way.

In order to overcome some of these emotional shields, a series of techniques have been developed. These range from the technique of *free association* by psychoanalysts, in which the client is encouraged to observe and speak about any thought that crosses his or her mind. These associations are then taken as material to be 'thought' about together. Slips of the tongue are also regarded as meaningful, and might give an indication of relevant inner world issues, as are dreams – the interpretation of which Freud called the 'Royal Road to the Unconscious'.

None of the above are, however, legitimate management or coaching tools and should not be elicited unless the client specifically brings them of his or her own volition. Even then, care needs to be taken not to cross the work boundary into a personal/therapeutic arena.

There is, however, one technique that is legitimate and effective in circumventing the well-established adult, conscious ways of hiding aspects of one's true self from oneself and from others. It is derived from work with children, and consists of asking the individual to draw a picture of their life: their past, their present, their future, their personal life and family and friends and hobbies, their work career, present-day issues, and future developments. And most importantly, no words. This injunction is because by the time most people reach midlife they are adept at spinning impressive webs of language, mission statements, strategic plans, etc. that often serve the purpose of partially, if not wholly, covering up what is really going on.

Asking for a picture alone to be drawn neatly sidesteps traditional modes of communication, and can often, at a glance, reveal issues of relevance to the understanding of the individual and the institution. For example, a picture of the workplace with barred windows looking to any outsider like a jail, a picture of the family with no sign of the father. Does this say something about the work–life balance? A picture with no past or no future; a picture that is drawn in a squared mathematical way, etc., etc. None of these examples are necessarily hard and fast evidence of anything, but they are useful opening gambits for a variety of topics concerning life and work. And, if coupled with 360-degree feedback forms and comments from family and friends, then the picture is often impressively clear. That does not mean that individuals cannot fall into states of vigorous denial, coming up with wondrous counter-interpretations of what is going on. When the process is, however, conducted in a small group of colleagues with everybody having a turn, as is the model at the Global Leadership Centre at the Insead International Business School at Fontainebleau, Paris, then the feedback is more likely to at least sink in, accompanied and facilitated, as it is, by the views of fellow members in the group.

The purpose of such feedback sessions is, importantly, not to expose or humiliate members – such as many fear before entering the process – but instead it is to help members to gain additional perspectives on their conduct and work. They will end up with a more 'rounded' picture, both in terms of acknowledging their skills and achievements, and also get some indications of areas that could do with further work. The goal is, ultimately, both personal and work-related improvement.

It would be unusual for individuals to obtain insights into their life and work that they hadn't come across before. But interventions such as those described above can give the individual, and sometimes the organization, a further nudge in the direction of action before it is too late.

A substantial help can be that of locating individuals, both in one's personal and professional life, to act as supporters or aides in the change process and authorizing them to act on their own understanding. Regular follow-up is essential for the new perspectives to have a chance to establish themselves. These meetings need to involve an assessment concerning whether the newfound ideas are relevant or not to personal, professional, and organizational life. If follow-up is minimal or ignored, then the likelihood is that the natural processes of denial and stabilization as exercised in the immediate past will resume the upper hand, and, as a consequence, learning will be minimal.

Both individuals and organizations generally pay enthusiastic lip service to the idea of growth and development whereas, in reality, these processes are experienced as unsettling, disturbing, and uncomfortable, and are thus often resisted with all our unconscious might.

Chapter 20

On the use of language

In formulating any hypothesis, or in pursuing the work that that hypothesis entails, it is far preferable to conduct the conversation in the *client's* language, idioms, and metaphors, rather than in your own. The former approach is much more likely to result in a process of new understanding as it is related to the past experience of the individual and organization, and, therefore, based on a more secure foundation. This is by contrast with 'educating' or 'pseudo-educating' them into your language, which will always have a 'foreign' element to it and, therefore, sit more artificially on past experience. It is likely to become a 'geological fault' between past and present, particularly at times of stress or pressure. Using the client's language also puts the consultant under appropriate pressure to see matters from another perspective rather than sticking to his or her own style.

Example

A chief executive, unprompted, brought a dream to a coaching session. In the dream, he had been going about his everyday business when all of a sudden a combine harvester (a large agricultural harvesting machine) appeared, apparently from nowhere, and pursued him at terrifying speed. This clearly represented a persecuting element of his life, specifically at work. From now on, the image of the 'combine harvester' was a much more real and lively description of elements at work that needed to be thought about and addressed than the somewhat fanciful language of 'persecutory anxiety'.

It is often so that leaders, managers, consultants, or coaches stick to their own language almost as a matter of professional dignity and worth. While this is understandable, there is a price to be paid for the habit. The price is that this language introduces difference and differentiation into the contact equation. There is substantial evidence that this 'caste system' of language does not foster cooperation – instead, it encourages a 'them and us' dynamic. Although I am not suggesting that one should create an impression of 'we're all the same', it equally needs to be understood, that to have a well-functioning organization, there has to be at least an *element* of 'we're all in the same boat, or flotilla of boats, travelling in the same direction'.

Chapter 21

On work–life balance

An appropriate work–life balance needs to be negotiated against the above-mentioned work cultural background of the company. The main reason for needing to have an appropriate work–life balance is to safeguard the mental and physical wellbeing of the individual, and thus to safeguard their capacity to make a positive and healthy contribution both at home and in the workplace.

Any ongoing imbalance in this home–work equation will result in negative consequences in one sector or the other, and sometimes in both. A 'workaholic' does neither himself, his family, nor his workplace any good, and sets a role model in all settings that is counterproductive – in fact, a role model of how-not-to behave. Going to work at 6.30 in the morning, and coming home at 11 pm, as well as bringing work home for the weekends, does not generally present any children at home with a model that they might wish to emulate in their adult life or even, for that matter, in their growing-up life.

Having a good work–life balance and taking holidays is not a form of self-indulgence that one should feel guilty about. It is a form of healthy self-maintenance that is essential for a competent fulfilment of personal and work roles.

Chapter 22

On stress

Stress is a common bugbear in relation to work. So what is it? Stress is the physical and mental sensation of being under pressure. How that is to be interpreted varies from individual to individual, and is related to their resilience or lack thereof. It is understood that stress has biological/physical as well as mental manifestations. The physical manifestations can take the form of increased irritability, raised blood pressure, heart attacks, as well as a multitude of psychosomatic conditions such as digestive problems, asthma, eczema, etc.

In mental states it can lead to restlessness, insomnia, as well as addictive behaviour – smoking, excess drinking of alcohol, the use of drugs, and so on. All the above physical and mental symptoms need to be seen as possible manifestations of work stress and need addressing. This might require a change in one's work patterns and work–life balance. It might require a change in one's eating and physical patterns – relaxation exercises, yoga, and related techniques may be helpful.

It further must be understood that stress is not a 'one person' symptom. At work, the contagion of stress can be transmitted into groups, from member to member, and throughout the system. This equally applies to family relationships. It, therefore, also needs to be thought about in a systemic way.

Nonetheless, it would be a mistake to see stress as entirely negative. A degree of stress acts as a spur to action; too much stress spoils the capacity for competent work.

As with most situations, denial is not a good way of dealing with institutional stress. The boss who says, 'we do not experience any stress in this organisation', expects to be complimented on his excellent 'running of the show'. In reality, he is illustrating his way of dealing or, for that matter, not dealing with stress. Stress in his organization is *verboten* – thus cannot be acknowledged, resulting in no measures being put into place to diminish it.

Example

Working in a premature baby unit with incubators full of babies just about clinging to life and wired up to a whole battery of instruments that measure the precariousness of the functioning of their biological systems is a stressful business.

Death is constantly lurking around the corner. Newborns in society represent the future and should bring joy and fulfilment. These bring the opposite.

In my experience consulting to them, the staff of such units are often young and female, and many are on the verge of having babies themselves. They, in a sense, are thus more vulnerable to the stress arising from their work than, say, their male colleagues and older women on the staff. They are, therefore, more susceptible to stress arising from their work. If they worked in the dermatology out-patient department of the same hospital, they might very well find themselves under less stress.

This type of stress is much more endemic in 'people' organizations than in others.

Example

A social worker working in a deprived community might very well come across day-to-day incidents of acute deprivation and abuse. The stress arising from such work can lead to substantial stress-related symptoms in the worker, including a 'blunting' of feeling and sensitivity that would result in the worker withdrawing into a cut off bureaucratic state of mind as a way of performing their task.

But what of a worker or the workforce of an organization that produces landmines, for example! Does one fall into a state of mind of being proud of the 'beauty' and effectiveness of one's product, or can one allow oneself to think about the hundreds and thousands of individuals who are maimed or killed by one's product?

Of course, there are other industries or professions in which matters are not as clear cut. What of the engineer who plans a dam that has substantial social and ecological consequences? Or someone in an industry that produces products that are open to abuse?

The standard response to these situations is not to think about it. Perhaps that is both necessary and inevitable. On the other hand, it needs to be recognized that these other factors are in the unconscious groundwater and foundations of the organization, and do have an effect on its dynamic. The tobacco industry might be seen as a good example of having been in denial for years in relation to the risks inherent in its products – not only in denial, but in active pursuit of activities intended to cover-up and deny the risks associated with its production.

In general, the work–life equation is skewed in the direction of work, and is presented in terms of workload, group pressure, etc. What is particularly depressing is that many organizations that have the most punishing routines for their staff have the most 'floral' policies about the values of family life, etc. The message of this hypocritical approach is clear. Work–life balance is all eyewash – we expect to squeeze the last drop of work possible out of you. The idea that one might get a better and more soundly based performance from a more balanced individual is a foreign idea in such organizations. As for those who embark on such punishing routines at work, the excuse is often that one needs to behave in such a manner 'until one is established', and after that one can change gear into a saner way of life. My observation is that the hoped-for saner way of life is very seldom achieved, and that such work patterns, once established, are likely to remain so for life.

The early establishment of these work patterns is often also paralleled by partner, family, and child-rearing patterns, where either both parents are working and child-rearing is delegated to a series of nannies or au-pairs, or to a pattern in which there is such a division of roles that the couple relationship is at risk of becoming emotionally sterile and marinated in resentment. The result, in some instances, is thus a welcoming of the work pressures, with their advantage of spending even less time at home with one's partner and children. Once one has been established in one's role in the firm as described above, a further cloud appears on the work and personal horizon: namely the so-called 'midlife crisis'.

Midlife here does not necessarily mean the middle of one's statistical life as counted in years, though it may be so. In effect, it means a certain state of mind in which one looks back – to where one has come from, both personally and, in this context, professionally – while at the same time looking ahead and speculating on what might lie there. The crisis partially involves fears over how this might affect oneself, as well as how one might manage it. This state of mind is often brought on by the growing old or dying of one's parents, the adolescence of one's children, and one's position in the professional pecking order at work. Is one going to get promotion, be made partner of the firm, etc.?

Midlife as a state of mind might stretch over quite a period of time and be dealt with in a variety of ways. At best, it is dealt with in a reflective thoughtful way involving all in one's network of life – partner, family, work colleagues, etc.

But, not uncommonly, the response is less reflective and more action based. This takes the form of taking flight from one's present state, with little thought to the consequences. The French artist Gauguin is a pertinent example, giving up his job as a clerk in a bank in Paris and heading off to Tahiti to paint. But not all midlife flights are as successful as his, and in general it is better to give some thought to the matter than to allow oneself to be carried along by the personal, societal, even hormonal, process that midlife entails.

The same question, of course, arises later in life, in relation to retirement. For some, the idea is taboo; it is the equivalent of death and not to be thought about. For others, it is something to be planned for in as realistic as possible a manner.

In working with groups of midlife top executives you get a range of responses to the question of retirement. Ask them to draw a picture of the future, and you often get a sketch of a couple sitting on deckchairs under a palm tree on an idyllic island.

How to get there, and the steps needed to reach that destination is another matter – very few have actually given thought to the transitional processes and how long it takes. It is regarded as something that will be dealt with when they are at retirement. In the meantime it is something that is put out of their mind.

In fact, it is a matter, like so many discussed above, that falls into the denial category in one's mind, for it entails two painful issues that people would rather avoid. The first is loss of identity. To a great many individuals their work role is a central pillar of their identity; strip that away, and they must now ask 'who am I?', or, more painfully, 'am I now a has-been?'. This state of mind affects not only the individual concerned, but also their family and personal networks.

For the transition to be well managed, time and thought are required, as do all transitions. Time to relinquish one's duties, time to take on the issues of the next phase of one's life.

The second painful issue that contributes to the denial of retirement is the perception of, and understanding that retirement, certainly in later years, ushers in the next and last phase of one's life, and looking ahead there is old age, possible infirmity, and eventually death.

Such matters are not comfortably held in one's mind as elements in one's everyday life. As a result, they are emotionally put aside, or possibly even totally denied.

Example

A beautiful example of this is the case of a very senior banker on the verge of retirement. He was referred for consultancy because, instead of reducing his hours at work, he had actually increased them and had a couch installed in his office. He often spent the night there. His ostensible reason was that he was responsible for financial links with a Far Eastern branch, and time differences made it essential for him to be at his desk for early morning trading.

In this instance, even his colleagues saw through this excuse and referred him for consultation. He did not take lightly to a dose of reality and the need to plan his transition out of his present role, but eventually got the point.

An avoidance of thought and planning about retirement has several consequences. A 'bridging' thought here, as part of the denial that there is a real problem to be dealt with, is the flight into pretending that retirement is actually the long holiday that had always been hoped for. Will travel the world, will have time to do what we've always wanted to do, hobbies, grandchildren, learning new languages, fishing, sailing, golf, dancing, watercolours – you name it, they'll plan it. Of course, there is some truth in this outlook and some, particularly those that have gradually embarked on some of these activities pre-retirement, do manage it, and manage it well. But mostly it must be seen as a manic de-fence against loss of identity, and denial of the feared 'bleakness' ahead.

It has been shown statistically that there is a disproportionately high incidence of death within six months of retirement. This is not because individuals retire on account of illness and then die. The reason is because of the above states of mind, and their influence on the mind–body equation. Again, there is clear evidence that at all ages, states of mind affect bodily function via hormonal and other biological pathways and vice-versa. The more the emotional up-set the greater the disturbance in the mind–body equation and the greater the chance of illness, accidents, and death.

It also needs to be remembered that retirement of one, or even both members of a couple, is an issue that needs to be emotionally worked through, and the problems to be met by both parties. In that regard, it is no different from the couple-work that is required from the arrival of a new baby, or the adolescence of their children. If there is a clear retirement policy and age in the company, there is at least a milestone on the horizon that cannot be avoided, and that can stimulate a relevant discussion at home and at work.

There are, however, exceptions to this rule. Sole individual practitioners can often go on without hindrance, and eventually create problems on account of their increasing senility, which is one way of trying to cheat retirement. More problematic is the matter of retirement in, say, a small family concern.

Example

Grandfather started the business, and he and grandmother and uncle Ernest are the sole shareholders. Grandfather has been going to the firm's offices and factory every morning at 8.00 am for the past 50 years, and is proud of never having taken a day off for sickness or for holiday. Various children and cousins have held jobs in the firm under grandfather's authority; some have failed, others survived; few have flourished.

The factory needs re-organization and re-capitalization in order to deal with a changing commercial environment and increased global competition. The managing director – father/grandfather – resists these suggestions with the support of the board – mother/grandmother and uncle. He also refuses to retire. Alternatively, he retires but still has his special parking place by the front door, his secretary of 30 years, and his office. The new managing director, his son, is still called young Mr …

The problem here is a double one: not only is there the issue of the denial of ageing and retirement, and of the need for 'young blood', but any move to force the 'old man' out of his company niche is emotionally – unconsciously – perceived as patricide – the killing of the father. The up and coming generation is thus caught in the no-man's land between the need for re-organization and the family credo of 'honour thy mother and father'. In circumstances like this, sadly on this occasion the only way open is for the business to go bust, and for all to be freed from their 'imprisonment'. In other more fortunate examples, non-family members are appointed and help the transition from a family concern into a more open-boundaried business.

In dealing with stress, the first element is undoubtedly the need for the individual to recognize that they are stressed. In my view there is no such creature as a 'non-stressed' individual. The latter is thus a stressed individual in a state of denial. Once the denial has been overcome, thought needs to be given as to the origins of the stress, along the lines outlined in this book. Most important, is to give some thought as to who there is in one's immediate personal or work environment who might help to keep one in touch and encourage one in this project of addressing issues. Asking for, and accepting, such help is a matter of generosity on both your side and theirs.

Chapter 23

Tackling 'below the surface' issues

There are a multitude of psychological concepts, theories, and frameworks that practitioners apply in thinking about and working with organizations. There are, however, a few key ones that are universally held, even though they are called by different terms. What follows is a basic toolkit that is of relevance in all organizations, at all times. These phenomena may occur singly, or in relation to others. For example, the mechanism of denial is often accompanied by the mechanism of projection.

Example

A factory is accused of having polluted a nearby stream. The management firmly denies that fact, while at the same time implying that the pollution comes from a rival factory upstream (denial and projection of blame onto others).

One of the most useful concepts is the concept of denial. In essence, it means that we refuse to take note of that which frightens us or points to our guilt, and instead pretend that everything is fine. The problem with this approach is that whereas in the short term it, perhaps, relieves us of anxiety, in the long term, denial, namely turning a blind eye to the matter, means that we cannot take whatever steps are necessary to work at addressing and remedying the matter. In the process, time is wasted and the problem gets worse.

Rivalry and competitiveness is an everyday personal and institutional dynamic. If, however, its existence is denied or, worse, covered up with politeness and sweet talk, then the rivalry manifests itself as an unconscious underground activity that results in non-cooperation and, at worst, sabotage and envious attacks. If, on the other hand, its existence is acknowledged, it can be seen as com-petitiveness in the open and thus be relieved of some of its 'toxicity'. Envy is a further important and relevant concept in the under-standing of organizational processes. Envy refers to a state of mind in which one wishes to have another's possessions or qualities. It is thus a two-person concept, and needs to be differentiated from jealousy which is a three-person concept. In jealousy one wishes to step into the shoes of another party in order to have a relation with the third. A husband might thus be jealous of his wife's lover.

Example

The deputy chief executive of an organization might be jealous of the closeness between the chief executive and his/her personal assis-tant and consequently behave is such a manner as to be rude to one or the other – in doing so damaging the overall functioning of the organization.

In this case, personal past dynamics thus interfere with present-day work reality.

Envy has different qualities. In small quantities, it can act as a stimulant. But it is fundamentally a destructive force. For example, looking at a man's Maserati car one might say to oneself, 'one day I'll have one of these'. Or, one might take the keys of one's own runa-bout out of one's pocket and scratch the paintwork of the Maserati. That would be an envious attack. 'If I can't have it, I will spoil it or ensure that no one else can enjoy it either'.

Example

A company director is impressed and consequently envious of a rival director whose department is thriving. Ideally one would hope that the two would cooperate and learn from each other. In an envious climate (determined, in part, by the personality of the former) the achievements of the latter are attacked, denigrated, and 'explained away'.

What, in this example, has been described in concrete terms also happens symbolically. Thus a colleague's good idea might be shot down as useless, not because it is so, but because, unconsciously, one wants to ensure that the person concerned does not gain an advan-tage in the institutional pecking order.

Aesop's fable of the fox and the sour grapes is an example of this everyday dynamic in public life. If one cannot reach something, in this case the longed-for grapes that hang too high up, one claims one doesn't want them because in any case they are supposedly sour.

Envy of someone else's status, beauty, competence, creativity, is an everyday event and ignored at one's peril.

Chapter 24

Matters of technique

But, as with many of the issues connected with attempting to read the unconscious subtitles, the question is what to do with one's hypotheses or interpretations of what might be going on. What is clear is what not to do. Providing what could be described as a 'simultaneous translation' is not called for. In fact, it would amount to the individual concerned being bombarded with a stream of ideas, many of which would come from that area of his or her mind that he or she would rather keep repressed.

It is, therefore, appropriate to read the unconscious subtitles as they appear, but when to feed them back, if at all, is a matter of judgement involving both timing and language.

As regards the timing of meetings with individuals, it is, in my view, important to state the time boundaries in which the work is to take place. It is often regarded as a generous and supportive thing to say 'take your time – we have as much time as you need', which is, at times, supportive of the task. But there is also another side to this issue.

When you go to the dentist, you know how much time you're booked in for that appointment. Half an hour, an hour, whatever has been agreed. You know that the time of discomfort will come to an end and when you will be 'released'. So what has this got to do with, say, a meeting with a member of staff? The member of staff may very well look forward to a meeting 'as long as it takes' to look at and deal with whatever work-related issues.

There is, however, something potentially anxiety-making and frightening at the thought of such a meeting – hence the dentist metaphor – and that to know when the time is up to leave the meeting can be reassuring in that regard. What is more, having a clear time structure enables both parties to time themselves as to what, and when, they want to raise relevant issues in the meeting.

From the point of view of the manager – if the meeting has a manager-type component to it – the manager can raise whatever potentially difficult matters there are in such a timed way that, once they are raised, there is sufficient time left in the meeting for them to be worked at in such a way that, when the member of staff leaves, both parties part with a good enough relationship and for the topic to be worked on in the interim between the present and the next meeting.

From the perspective of the employee in the room, the clear time boundaries, as mentioned, give not only the assurance that one might escape relatively unscathed from the ordeal, but also the possibility that anything problematic could be left to the very end of the meeting, at which point one might make one's 'escape'. In this way, one avoids the possibility of having to stay and deal with the matter, at least for the time being. It also allows for the possibility of illuminating 'hand on the door-handle' types of communication-cum-flight. This is not uncommon, and allowance must be made for such a dynamic in everyday ongoing work relationships.

Part 4

Practical and technical matters

Chapter 25

Institutions and their management

As is clear from the previous chapters there is no way of being either personally or professionally engaged without the concept of there being an institution in which one has, or is assumed to have, direct membership. One is thus directly subject to the concrete and psychological principles and matters of how the institution is led or managed. This in turn is influenced by the factors mentioned in earlier chapters.

There needs to be serious thought given as to what function (primary and related tasks) the institution concerned is there to perform and whether the in-house mechanisms for leading or management are appropriately in place.

The central point to this enquiry has to be whether enough account is given to the risks involved in the activities of the organization. One only has to look at the business pages of the papers to read that a great many businesses run on the basis of wishful thinking and thus are deeply mired in an atmosphere of denial. And this includes so-called win–win arrangements which also operate on the basis of denial.

This way of functioning – namely denial of the reality of life – is, of course, very attractive in a psychological sense and thus has a 'magnetic' pull toward membership of this group. Hence the regular appearance of pyramidal financial schemes, the pseudo-growth and success of Enron or Parmalat, including the auditors who too are sucked in.

In order to avoid falling into the trap of membership of the group process it helps to have a personal reference group with whom your experience of self and the 'magnetic' group can be discussed and seen in perspective.

This process has been effective in the airline business with pilots and staff being encouraged to share their problems with colleagues. Previously denial was proposed for so-called reasons of legal procedures.

The same openness is now encouraged in the health services where staff are encouraged to bring their issues to regular meetings called Schwartz Rounds, with colleagues.

It takes courage to 'fess up' to one's failings and mistakes but makes it possible for self and others to learn from them.

The basic principle is thus one of being in touch with reality and to avoid stuffing more worms into one's own internal psychological 'sludge pits' which overflow into emotional and psychological outlets including personal relationships, children's states of mind, and even the family dog!

Chapter 26

Commerce and its taboos

A 'taboo', by definition, is a subject that cannot be raised and, therefore, certainly not debated. The reason for this state of mind is the belief that if the taboo is broken 'all hell will break loose'. It is the modern equivalent of the Greek myth of 'Pandora's Box'. In the story, once the box is opened it is never possible to get all the world's evils back in again, and life's equilibrium will be destroyed forever. A further sobering tale, is that of Cassandra. It was Cassandra's fate that she could foretell the future but that nobody would believe her. Both these myths provide food for thought in relation to the contents of this book. Could it be that underlying our whole way of life – personal, work-related, and societal, we are in denial about the consequences of the way we are conducting ourselves for us, our lifestyle, work, society, and the environment?

The Oxford Dictionary defines 'exploiting' as 'use for one's own advantage, and their disadvantage'. It is a matter of debate whether our and the world's 'lifestyle', as a whole, is based on this philosophy or not, but it seems reasonable to at least puncture the taboo surrounding this topic. The present-day 'Cassandra' response is to deny any exploitative elements at all. In fact, to the contrary – goings-on are presented as being in the service of *enhancing* the quality of life of the world's population. While there is, no doubt, an element of truth in this perspective, it could also be seen as a denial of the facts: the exploitation of human and natural resources, and the accompanying greed. Greed is, at times, presented as good in the business world. Concern about employment conditions and the environment, by contrast, are traditionally seen as 'wet', liberal, and out of touch – in denial of everyday commercial reality. Although many companies today claim attempts to 'go green' on a large scale, the day-to-day functioning may completely ignore this endeavour – lights left on all night, recyclables thrown in with general rubbish, etc. The difficulty is that with such polarization – greed good, welfare bad – it is hard to get any sort of constructive debate going, not about the planet and whether it needs saving, but how to conduct oneself in one's business affairs and in managing and leading one's organization.

An organization that has an 'exploitative' philosophy may very well be successful in the short term. However, whether such functioning is of benefit to it in the longer term is a matter of debate. It is probably worthwhile to consider what an 'ecologically sound', in both a mind and environmental sense, business might look like, and following that to evaluate whether one might wish to make changes to how one's own business is to run.

There are several layers of activity that need to be looked at:

1. The nature of the product or service involved and its effect on the environment. Has thought been given to this? Have steps been taken to reduce or minimize the negative effects of one's activity? There are no doubt a multitude of examples, from extracting water from an aquifer to produce soft drinks and thereby lowering the water table to the detriment of local farmers. We may also think about the production of landmines and the effect of these on the civilian population. The standard response here is, 'if we don't make them our competitor will' which is true enough, but probably not good enough a reason to avoid giving *any* thought to the problem, as so often happens.

2. Exploitation of labour. At worst labour is regarded as a disposable product that can be 'squeezed' and then discarded. It doesn't make for an effective workforce and perhaps more importantly, it absolutely suppresses any creativity in the workforce.

Chapter 27

Some thoughts on business schools

It needs to be remembered that business schools are businesses run by business men or women who sell a product. What is the product they sell? Education! But there are many ways of describing the above function. Business schools are excellent at creating networks for students and graduates. They are good at fostering a climate of confidence in students about their position in society as alumni. Both of these qualities are highly valued emotionally and financially.

There is also the matter of teaching versus learning. The teaching often takes the form of members being literally 'bombarded' with case histories of global companies, or from prestigious business schools. How much of this can be, or is, actually applied, by students back home in their work situation is questionable. Top teachers from all over the world are hired as staff, or jet in from elsewhere, to create stunning performances for the students. The teachers are then given ratings by the students and they, in turn, provide feedback. In a recent four-week course of 70 students, the ratings were 95% at the five (top mark) level. Is this rating truly possible in a learning environment, or are we perhaps, instead, talking about a group phenomenon of mutual idealization? In this situation, the Deans are, of course, delighted, for good 'word of mouth' feedback is essential for recruitment and business. But is this *learning* – in the sense of change within individuals in relation to both work and personal matters? In advanced management or leadership programmes, the members are often mostly in the 'midlife' range of personal and work experience. They are often sent to 'brush up their expertise' en route to top jobs, or to pick up the 'latest tricks of the trade' in the business. Once on the course they soon realize the previously unspoken tasks that need addressing. These are namely, reviewing their life to date, and thinking about their future, and remaining personal and professional life. Many business school professors regard the above as subsidiary to their programmes or as 'wet' partially because in their careers they never 'worked at the coal face' or had coaching. As in many other professions, the focus becomes one of impressing one's colleagues with learned papers which results in neglecting the needs of the actual clients.

Chapter 28

The board, the CEO, and the management

Relationships between the board, the CEO, and the management can be helpful to all, but can also be highly problematic if the boundaries between the various aspects of the organization are unclear. The most common problem is usually the relationship between the chair of the board/president, and the chief executive officer/director. Who runs the show? If the president feels he/she does, this might seriously undermine the CEO. If the latter is in charge, the question arises of 'what is the role of the president?' The most effective role of managing the relationship is for the president and board to provide an umbrella under which the CEO and the management group run the show. This 'umbrella function' is in part to represent and protect the organization in its functioning with the outside world, while being sufficiently engaged in, and informed about, the inner functioning of the organization. From the above it is clear that a regular, ongoing, on-task relationship between the two office bearers, and layers of the organization, is essential. In this 'couple' relationship the dynamics to be expected are thus – as with any 'marital' relationship – relatively harmonious cooperation versus deep rivalry. One way organizations have of dealing with this issue is to have the president and CEO roles fused into one individual. That can make for supposedly effective functioning, but it has the disadvantage of there being only one 'head'. Should something go wrong it leaves the organization 'headless' in more senses than one. It also makes for a degree of loneliness that is hard to bear. Furthermore, there is the risk to the individual and the organization if they fall into a state of charismatic leadership, which is fine while it lasts, but can result in catastrophic consequences when departure or retirement looms.

It is, therefore, an integral part of the role of the leader to make sure that the organization is always in a fit state for a planned or unexpected transition. As mentioned previously, much has been written about leadership styles. In my view the most toxic of these is the combination of charisma and narcissism, in which the leader uses all available resources in the service of promotion of self and self-image, with resultant neglect of colleagues, staff, and the organization as such.

Chapter 29

On meetings and their management

In a meeting, the chair's role is to facilitate the pursuit of the agenda, to maintain and set time boundaries, to encourage contributions from members by damping down on the overbearing participants and encouraging the silent ones. The role is essentially a leadership one that facilitates and contains the group process. In so doing, the chair ensures that the meeting is working to task and accessing the views of the members. By implication this means that the chair role must take precedence over the chair's role as member of the meeting, or of other roles held at other times in the same organization. This matter can be clarified by the chair saying, 'speaking in my role as chair' or 'speaking in my role as X', whatever other role the chair of the meeting might hold in the organization.

In order for a meeting to run in an ordered work-orientated way with a minimum of anti-task unconscious behaviour, it needs to be structured and contained. Secure boundaries are necessary, with no external disruption or to-ing and fro-ing. There needs to be clarity with time boundaries, both as regards starting and finishing times. There needs to be clarity of membership – who is expected to attend, and who not.

There also needs to be clarity about the agenda and what is expected of members, what to note, what needs deciding on, what needs to be taken from the meeting and acted on, by whom, and by what deadline.

Thought needs to be given to the construction of the agenda, who determines what is on the agenda, and what preparatory work is required before items appear on the agenda.

A competent agenda will allow for a certain beginning time for the work to get underway, followed by any difficult and contentious items, and then end with agreed, designated and timed action paragraphs for the future.

It is a common institutional process for difficult items, consciously or unconsciously, to be put at the bottom of the agenda, and, therefore, there 'not being enough time' at the end of the meeting for these matters to be addressed. And so a process of avoiding and evading difficult decisions is embarked on, to the detriment of the functioning of the organization.

The unconscious process of there not being enough time in the meeting to deal with contentious issues is usually achieved in one of two ways. Either the agenda is packed with enough 'padding' of relatively unimportant matters that could equally well be dealt with elsewhere (sometimes put on the agenda in order not to hurt the feelings of worthy members of the 'congregation' whose hobby-horse is that particular agenda item). A rigid pruning and planned pacing of the agenda is thus necessary in order to avoid this dynamic.

Another way of 'achieving' running out of time is for there to be such an intense discussion of early agenda items that there is not enough time to reach the later contentious items. In politics this is called filibustering. This usually takes the form of abusing one or other of the usual early agenda items, for example, minutes of the last agenda meeting. One might hear intense quibbling about words, or on what was decided last week. The 'pinnacle' of such behaviour is often taken by individuals who were not present at the last meeting, and who then come up with comments like 'I don't agree with that decision'. To deal with this sort of objection, there needs to be absolute clarity about what the constitutional requirements are for the taking of a decision (two thirds? three quarters? unanimous?). If the constitution says unanimous, it, by definition, means that any one member has a veto, and can thus put a halt to any proceedings.

In my experience, unanimous decisions are either taken about matters of little importance, often fall apart behind the scenes, or are sabotaged. Even though a decision is on the verge of being unanimously agreed, it is worthwhile, in addition, enquiring whether there are additional elements or perspectives that need to be taken into consideration – thus making for a 'unanimous decision' but with the possibility of 'work in progress' as opposed to permanent foreclosure of the topic.

The second 'trick' to delay progress down the list of agenda items is to pick on the commonly occurring early agenda item of 'any other related matters'. This opens the door to a whole variety of possible items that can be stretched out to fill any amount of time. The enthusiastic discussion of such agenda items is, in my view, evidence of an unconscious group process in which all members take part, in the service of avoiding the problematic items on the agenda. Further evidence comes in the response of the members when such a dynamic is pointed out. Hurt that one should assume such base motives about their behaviour, 'all they are doing' is addressing an urgent matter to hand.

Example

A further 'trick' in the undermining and anti-task stakes is as follows: a task might have been delegated to a sub-committee, often representing particular skills in law, finance, technical matters, for example. That committee has been asked to make recommendations and to bring these back to the main body. When this is done the 'trick' is to take no notice of the brief that was given, the work that has been done and the subsequent recommendation. 'Experts' spring up in the main body of the committee like weeds in a neglected garden. All the work comes to nothing; the sub-committee is demoralized, annoyed, and reluctant to take on further tasks. The overall result is that the problem is added to the already formidable pile of other issues.

In order for a meeting to run to task, which is to address the duties and functions that the meeting is there to perform, attention needs to be given to how that is to be achieved: as mentioned previously, attention needs to be given to the setting, the seating, the time allocated, as well as the agenda. Agendas and accompanying material need to be circulated well in advance for the individual members to have an opportunity to inform themselves of relevant matters. This advice about how to go about things is so obvious that it would appear offensive to even mention it, were it not for one fact: it seldom happens. Material is sent out late, and sometimes even tabled. This is supposedly on account of 'business, workload, and pressure' or some such similar reason.

It is, however, worthwhile to consider another possibility: that the committee is essentially seen as a rubber-stamping device for decisions already taken elsewhere. It is, therefore, *not* important for the members of the committee to have the relevant information and, at that, time to study it, and to think about its implications. At the same level, this handling of the committee suits both parties engaged in the process well. The 'decision makers' elsewhere don't have to bother with debate and questioning, the members of the committee don't have to bother much with the material presented to them, nor do they have to embark on the possible 'uncomfortableness' of questioning the material and debating alternatives. It also saves them from revealing their embarrassing lack of understanding of the issues, while ensuring their continued role, status and remuneration.

The reader might feel offended by my implying the implementation of consciously devious methods of management and leadership. Nothing could be further from the truth! It is, of course, possible that the occasional deviant follows that pathway. No! What I am implying is the presence of *unconscious* mechanisms of which the parties are unaware. It is only when space is given for the thought and acknowledgement that such processes can, and regularly do, occur that something can be done to reduce their presence and 'toxicity'.

It suits both parties well, and can thus be seen as a form of passive and relatively thoughtless dependence on a leader practising either an authoritarian or charismatic leadership style. Again, one could argue that the above is a cynical description of a relatively rare occurrence. Given a moment's observation of working practices and events in one's own organization, however, goes some way towards realizing that matters aren't perhaps as 'squeaky clean' or clear as one had hoped for, or imagined.

What I have been describing are pretty much everyday dynamics that we all, to a degree, are vulnerable to. That is different from a more 'toxic' form of management, known colloquially as the 'mushroom' theory of management. As with growing mushrooms for the supermarkets, it is based on the methodology of 'keep them in the dark and feed them horseshit', the 'thems', in this case, being either the board or committee members. This way of going about things borders on fraudulent behaviour, and is the very basis of many fraud cases revealed in the business pages of newspapers and economic journals.

In leading a group of individuals as described above, it is extremely helpful if the chair of the meeting has an awareness of the parameters of design and behaviour that make for a good meeting, as well as having an eye open for the various unconscious and anti-task behaviours that might manifest themselves. 'Forewarned is forearmed', as the expression goes.

If the above parameters of structuring and chairing are followed, they give the best chance of the meeting being on-task, covering its agenda and drawing on the expertise and wisdom of the individuals sitting around the table.

By contrast, a boundary-less, unstructured group open to disruption, with individuals reading their smartphones on their laps, or texting, or taking disruptive phone-calls, can result in only one thing: an anti-task meeting that can in no way draw upon the talents and expertise of the membership. In addition, such meetings also have a tolerance for substitute members being sent to take the place of those that for one or another, often dubious, reason cannot be present. This results in a rolling membership with little continuity of the thought and process that is required in a well-functioning group. An 'as if' group will only produce 'as if' results of management and leadership.

Chapter 30

Practical issues affecting meetings

The seating arrangements to some extent determine the relationship between office bearers and members, and also member/member relationships. Serried rows create dependency (and rebellion?) while a circle implies equality of membership. A central table or tables signify a work orientation. There should be the correct number of chairs for the number of individuals expected. An assortment of different chairs will imply a 'pecking order' of the participants and thus influence the decision. The Chairperson should ensure that meetings are 'contained' both in the sense of being free of external interruption and held within the allocated time boundaries. The degree of confidentiality expected of members for the meeting overall, or for its agenda components, needs to be clearly spelt out.

In the construction of the agenda it is advisable for potentially contentious items to be placed in the body of the agenda. Placing them too early in the sequence can overshadow and contaminate the entire meeting, too late runs the risk of 'running out of time' and the item being 'buried'. In covering agenda items it is advisable for the chair to spell out what the matters are that need discussion and decision, as opposed to being noted for information.

In summary, the assumption in meetings is always that matters are dealt with in a conscious and rational manner. The reality is different. It is, therefore, wise to look at not only what is said, but also to attempt to elicit what is not being said. Equally important is to consider what is intended and how such matters might be misinterpreted – thus giving an opportunity of minimizing the damage.

Part 5

Coaching, consultancy, and related matters

Chapter 31

On consultancy – benefits and risks

As mentioned earlier it is often a good idea to get an outside, competent, neutral person to 'cast an eye' over the organization and its functioning. In some specific 'technical' areas, such as law, elements of finance, particular production methods etc., it is important to get an expert in these areas. But overall the 'expertise' required is one of astute observation: the capacity to get on and communicate across boundaries, and to present ideas and hypotheses in a facilitating and non-persecutory way. In these instances, it is often better to engage someone *out* of the area of expertise in the observed organization, thus reducing the risk of preconception.

The main benefit of consultancy is to get an external, hopefully independent, perspective on the organization and its practices. One thus needs to differentiate between out-of-house consultancy and in-house consultancy, the latter being carried out by a member of the organization itself to be consulted to. In this case, the independent perspective is likely to be compromised, but to what degree depends, to an extent, on the size of the organization and the base within the organization of the independent consultant.

An external consultant, by contrast, is independent, though there is still the risk of a degree of dependence on account of the fact that the consultant's livelihood, to a lesser or possibly major degree, depends on the proceeds of the consultancy contract.

An independent consultant thus comes with, and is contracted for, a specific brief. In some instances they are hired for their specific skills, say a tax consultant or an engineering consultant, where it is expected that they will bring specific skills and facts that are not, or are to a lesser degree, available in-house.

Most consultants, however, are hired to investigate, report on, and solve specific problems within the organization. They are thus invited to observe its functioning and, interview, if appropriate, the staff. In my view, the state of mind at the beginning of this process is one of a visiting anthropologist. You're allowed into the group, or tribe, or organization; you're part of it, but also not; you can observe its functioning, and, most importantly, you can ask questions about what is going on and why. In so doing, you are raising issues that have perhaps not been thought about or questioned for a long time. At this phase of work my favourite definition of consultancy is 'Licensed Stupidity'.

In looking at the functioning of the organization, it also often becomes clear that what they say they do, and what they actually do, are divergent activities, often widely so. In that case, it becomes a question of focussing which activities are in the service of the primary task of the organization and which are not.

It also often becomes clear that the supposed problem you were called in to look at is not the problem at all. Alternatively, and most often, it is instead, a 'symptom' of wider issues that are either not known, or, more commonly, denied. This then requires a careful 'diplomatic' renegotiation of the work to be done. This is best done at one of the periodical reviews scheduled as part of the process of monitoring the work of the consultant through the medium of 'ongoing working notes'.

Chapter 32

The consultant role

The hoped-for, possibly unconscious, assumption held by one as potential consultant is that your appointment is based on a thought-through and competent assessment of your qualities and skills as held up to the client's needs and problems. That may well be so. But other possibilities must also be borne in mind. At one end of the spectrum is the hope and wish that you are capable of working miracles, can solve the problem in no time at all, and at no cost to them emotionally or organizationally – that you will perform a sort of messianic saviour intervention. This is not very likely, but there are a variety of messianic figures in the consultancy field who command large fees and thrive on their messianic reputation. Having performed their messianic intervention they move on, often leaving the client bereft and looking for the next available messiah.

At the other end of the spectrum is the possibility that you have been chosen with the unspoken, and at times unconscious, assumption that you are the least likely to cause much upheaval and 'damage' by your intervention, and can, therefore, be let loose in the organization without too much risk of disruption or change. Particularly in instances where there is substantial ambivalence about the consultancy programme, it is not unusual to hire a 'tame' or 'lame' consultant, thus proceeding with the consultancy in apparently real terms, but not in spirit. In this case we are thus talking about an auditioning process in which the choice is made on the basis of choosing the least threatening consultant. 'We really liked the consultants and got on really well' might mean 'we have found someone who is readily available for mutual idealisation'.

A further possible negative dynamic at this stage is to hire a plethora of consultants, all working at different tasks in different venues and settings, so that no coherent overall picture can or does emerge.

The work of the many consultants is, in this scenario, as disconnected with each other as the cooperation between the units and sub-units being consulted to. The end result is the creation of a 'mirror image' of un-connectedness that parallels the problems of the organization but does nothing to resolve the institutional problems.

The key question that, of course, needs to be asked at the beginning phase of a consultancy is why now – why not six months previously or next year? This often flushes out the hidden dynamics of the institution that determine the timing. Matters that affect the timing are often issues such as the secret illness or family dynamics of senior office bearers, a change in the legislation affecting the business, guilt at leaving the organization and, therefore, unconsciously embarking on bringing in a 'caretaker' who would enable those leaving to do so in a quieter and less disruptive manner.

Relating the matter of timing as to when a consultant is hired and the taking and implementation of difficult decisions, is a central part of leadership. This can be in stark contrast to the tendency of some leaders to retain their favourable, loved, self-image in the organization. It is thus understandable that a consultant is at that point hired to make the obvious recommendations, leaving the existing management with the opportunity to 'wring their hands' in distress at these 'monstrous recommendations' while putting all the blame on the consultant and the brutal philosophy espoused by his or her consultancy organization.

The question of why this consultant, why now, and with what expectation, is one that needs to be asked, not only by the consultant concerned but also by those that commission the consultancy. As implied above, the calling in of a consultant is often an avoidance of in-house decision-making, and in doing this is potentially an undermining of the authority and competence of in-house management and leadership structures.

There is thus a two-fold risk to the organization of calling in a consultant. At a conscious level it might undermine the existing management structures, and create opportunities for a splitting process to be enacted along the lines of playing off one's parents against each other in order to achieve one's goals. In this case it would be a case of playing off the consultant against the management – sometimes by inviting the consultant unconsciously to head a rebellious 'cabal' against the existing establishment.

Example

The president of a large company is under massive pressure from his wife. She is fed up with the family's ex-pat status and wishes to return to their homeland. The president feels that to leave his position at that point would undermine his role, the company's future, and possibly damage his bonus. Hiring a forceful external consultant who takes over and allows the president to take a 'back-seat' and thus quietly and unobtrusively to slide out of his dilemma is one way of supposedly dealing with the problem.

Example

A head of a company has been told that she has invasive cancer and not long to live. She prefers not to let it be known and instead hires a consultant who acts – perhaps unknowingly – as a buffer from reality so that the head can resign graciously. If, in this scenario, the consultant does not have the knowledge of what is really going on, the consultancy work might very well focus on lesser peripheral issues rather than on the need for a transition in the leadership of the company.

Example

A change in legislation casts major doubts on the functioning and future of the company. The company staff are not aware of the implications of the changes. The director of finance is crucially aware. Appointing a consultant to perform an intervention of one kind or another makes for a 'smoke screen' behind which the director can make an elegant departure.

There is also the question of by what authority the consultant is in the organization. To put in another way, who has the authority to invite a consultant in, and what subsequently happens to the consultancy in the organization?

It is clear that whoever invites the consultant into the organization must have the backing of the authority vested in him or her to do so. Thus a junior employee would not have the authority, whereas a branch manager might have, though perhaps only once they have checked with 'them above'.

But it is not only a matter of getting the go-ahead from 'higher echelons' of the organization; it is also important for the 'lower echelons' to be informed of the intention of the intervention. It is, therefore, advisable to get some form of sanction from the membership. This, at least, would go some way in reducing the suspicions of the workforce as to what the management is up to. For there is always the unspoken fear in the membership that the consultant is a secret, or not so secret, agent of the management, and, on the other hand, the fear in the management that the consultant will 'go native' and lead a 'Che Guevara' type of movement against management.

Given these dynamics, it is essential for the consultant not to 'fraternise' with the members of the organization at whatever level. For the ultimate unconscious purpose of the 'fraternisation' is not usually social or supportive, but could be seen instead as an attempt to get the consultant to become 'one of us' and to see things from 'our perspective'; be on 'our side'.

The consultant is thus at risk of not only losing their independent status, but also of being seen as becoming partisan to one or other grouping within the organization.

For the consultant to maintain their independent perspective and status, it is essential that standards and boundaries of confidentiality are spelt out right from the start of the intervention, and strictly adhered to. I am not prescribing coldness, unfriendliness, or 'academic detachment', but it needs to be made clear that this is the most professional way of proceeding in one's work as consultant.

It is equally important for there to be regular feedback to all levels of the organization, on agreed lines of confidentiality. General themes and specific issues may both need to be addressed, without any issues being traceable to specific individuals.

Both the authority to do the work and the sanction to participate must be constantly kept in mind. Regular reports, preferably in the form of three or six monthly 'working notes', are desirable. This should amount to a continuous process of enquiry, implementation, and dialogue with the various sectors of the organization.

All members of the organization would ideally maintain a 'consultancy participant' state of mind. This creates a commonly held set of questions, for the individual and the group, of 'what is going on here, is it relevant to our work and our organization's future, and what are we going to do about it?'

This differs from a style of consultancy in which the consultants go about the organization with a 'pen and clipboard' state of mind, resulting in a definitive report. In the former style, the focus is on the members of the organization observing and enquiring, and taking a degree of responsibility for continuing this process after the consultants have left. In the latter, the members are given a diagnosis and a prescription. It is often assumed that this will be implemented in the absence of the consultant who made the recommendation in the first place.

I have previously mentioned the risk of role confusion between consultant and in-house management. This a risk for both the organization and the consultant. The 'visiting anthropologist' consultant observes and feeds back hypotheses to the organization, along with questions of how the issues arising may be addressed. When the role of 'visiting anthropologist' is forgotten, the consultant may, instead, be seduced into the role of an idealized figure, someone who could lead the organization more effectively than its existing leadership. This is understandably tempting. The offer may be played into by existing management who wish to 'abandon ship' for a variety of reasons but cannot. For example, they may fear accusations of treachery, or simply feel too much guilt. Therefore, the combination of 'escaping leader' and 'idealised consultant' forms a powerful collusive dynamic.

That is not to say that this dynamic always ends in tears. The fundamental issue in this case is that decisions are made on the basis of deep-down personal and institutional unconscious desires, rather than on the basis of an open discussion about the best outcome for the organization and its strategic horizons.

Once the process has started, how should one conduct oneself as consultant and consumer of consultancy? Primarily, one must respect and acknowledge the difference in these two roles. The consumer is available for consultant intervention as they go about their everyday business. The consultant, in turn, goes about their business of *enquiry*. A central part of the consultancy process is to form tentative hypotheses as to what is going on in both the conscious and unconscious processes at work in the organization. These hypotheses need both to be anchored in the primary task of the organization, and to relate to the issues for which consultancy has been requested.

The formulation of these hypotheses, their testing, and subsequent implementation are the product of a joint effort between staff and consultant. The phrase 'action research' could describe this function. As a wise colleague once put it, 'you flirt with a hypothesis, you don't marry it'. If one does 'marry' a particular hypothesis, it may foreclose the capacity to see other relevant issues at play.

The advantage of this method is that any recommendations that arise are already based in the 'body and mind' of the organization. Furthermore, any ambivalence about the consultation should be out in the open – available for working on towards resolution or acceptance. When the consultant leaves, the process is established in the 'bones' of the organization, thus enhancing the chances that the work will continue.

If there is a follow-up consultation, the established way of proceeding can be resurrected. This also avoids the possibility of an emotionally unworked-through process report being issued at the end.

When such reports are issued, it can feel as if the organization and its members have been subjected to a school examination or criminal investigation. The organization is either left with the task of implementation by its own means and devices, or else offered a second tranche of consultancy work for implementation.

The post-consultancy implementation is often not embarked upon. The recommendations are, instead, 'kicked into the long grass'. The 'elegant' way of doing this is to express one's thanks and to say: 'we understand the situation and will get on with it'. In effect, nothing happens and the organization carries on in its well-trodden sterile path.

When implementation is, instead, phase two of the consultancy, the risk arises of a state of mind of undue dependency on the consultant. The organization makes itself only passively available for change.

At an unconscious level, this suits both parties. Because it is up to the consultants, to do the work, the organization can 'relax'. It also suits the consultants because they have a dependent audience who do not question their processes. In this case one might expect robust interchanges as part of the implementation process.

In embarking on an organizational consultancy it is essential for both the consultant and the organization to maintain a systemic perspective. Wherever the entry point is into the organization and whatever arises in the area under investigation, it is important to remember that it is part of a whole system. However relevant the issues are to a specific setting, any hypothesis and intervention should include the overall perspective.

This is a perspective that is denied at one's peril. I described earlier how 'Fred' was seen as a key problem but actually functioned as a 'pit canary', bringing to light important suppressed group issues, in an executive group. The same dynamic can occur in organizational consultancy. Being called in to consult to a specific department, sales or the outpatient department, for example, may well be an appropriate starting point. However, the problems they are experiencing might only be the 'tip of the iceberg'. The entire iceberg, in fact, might need consultation, and, if so, particular attention should be paid to areas beneath the surface of the water.

This realization often comes as unwelcome news to the organization. It is more comfortable to have a 'scapegoat' for that allows oneself to sit back in a detached, self-righteous state of mind, than to participate in a review process.

Example

A clinical case. A children's department of a psychological service noticed that a steady stream of children were referred from a specific school with 'bullying conduct disorders'. All the referrals were sound enough in themselves, but the experienced staff noted that there wasn't any evident reason why this particular school should have more of this sort of problem than other schools serving a similar catchment area. Discussions with a group of the teachers soon revealed a style of management by the headteacher that was both bullying and disruptive. The problem was an organizational one in which the referred youngsters were merely the tip of the proverbial iceberg. In the institution, there was an endemic atmospheric issue in which bullying could not be dealt with at any level.

In this case, both the school and the head structures were amenable to an intervention, and, with time, the organizational climate changed. The number of referrals for bullying fell to normal community levels.

When looking at organizational issues systemically it might be helpful to think of a mosquito buzzing around, looking for a suitable victim. Once bitten, the victim may succumb to malaria or dengue fever, or may only suffer an irritating itch – depending on what the mosquito is carrying.

The mosquito represents the unconscious organizational problem looking for a receptacle to express itself. The victim represents the individual or organizational subset most vulnerable to this problem. 'Organisational mosquitoes' are always present, even in the best-run organizations, and it is inevitable that certain individuals and groupings will be susceptible to their bites.

Susceptibility could be based on any number of predisposing factors. These may include unresolved issues from the past. An individual with complicated inner world parental relations may be more likely to be stirred-up into an anti-management state of mind, in which management represents an emotional successor to the parental function.

Equally, certain subsets of a global concern might be more vulnerable to a scapegoated state of mind due to problematic cultural stereotyping, or because of the nature of their particular products.

The great temptation, however, is to see problems as having a specific site and boundary, it is essential to ask whether there is not also a systemic component.

Chapter 33

Coaching – 'sin bin' or learning opportunity

The same issues apply to coaching. Why has this particular individual been sent for coaching, or asked for coaching? It may be for valid developmental reasons, but it is always worth considering that the individual concerned might represent an aspect of organizational dynamics. The systemic process, therefore, may also need to be addressed at the organizational level.

In the early days of coaching it was quite common for individuals to be sent for 'remedial' coaching. 'Would you please see X for coaching – he has problems with Y'. The coachee him or herself was often resistant to the process and saw it as a form of punishment or probation. Often, the individual was 'not fitting in' to the institutional culture. While this may be a problem, the coachee maintaining a level of individuality may provide a creative 'breath of fresh air' to an institution that needs – but refuses – to 'inhale'.

Had it existed at the time, would Galileo have been sent for coaching? Was the Spanish Inquisition a crude and violent form of remedial coaching to make 'misfits' into acceptable group members?

Thankfully, much coaching nowadays is developmental as it is recognized that encouraging in-house talent is one of the most effective and economical ways of 'growing the business'.

How should this form of coaching be conducted? Perhaps it is best to think of what should not be done. The dynamic should not be one in which the coach 'knows best' and tells the coachee what to do in a form perhaps closer to indoctrination than coaching.

Coaching should create a secure, confidential space to which the coachee can bring the thoughts and feelings that perhaps do not have a space and time in the everyday work timetable and routine. 'Tiredness can kill' scream the motorway electronic signboards – 'take a break'. 'Routine work and stress can cause dullness – take a coaching break' might be the equivalent organizational message.

The coaching space should give the opportunity to 'take a break' from the everyday and to look at events from a different perspective. It should also be a chance to give credence and thought to peripheral or emotional matters that, in the hurly-burly of everyday life, are perhaps pushed aside.

It used to be thought that emotions should be seen as an interference in the thinking process and should be put out of one's mind. It is now recognized that emotions are a core element of the thinking process, and should, therefore, be valued for their contribution to mental activity. Old habits, however, die-hard, and emotions are still regularly regarded as a nuisance and an irrelevance.

Coaching provides a private and confidential opportunity to explore emotions related to one's work role and to consider how far they influence one's professional behaviour. It may also become clear that the same dynamics have an echo in one's personal life and conduct. Personal revelations, however, that should perhaps be seen as a beneficial side effect of the coaching and not the primary reason for which the firm is paying.

Coaching allows haphazard non-thinking. It is a slot in which adventurous, emotional thoughts can make their appearance, and some thought can be given to the motivation behind them. Crucially, the role of the coach is to provide a contained and confidential space to encourage whatever thoughts surface, and to work with the client in finding the meaning and application of the mental material spread out before them.

It is common to find that the more one is stuck in a particular state of mind, or pre-occupied with a specific problem, the harder it is to stand back and consider different options. A helpful coach could raise the possibility that what is presented might be perceived from a variety of viewpoints. When seen from one perspective, a problem might feel insurmountable. Yet, viewed from another way, new and fruitful interpretations may appear.

Coaching, if well conducted, gives the opportunity to give up, at least for a time, a particular fixed way of seeing things and to allow the coachee to consider a different approach. While the fixed idea may not in itself be wrong, it suggests that the coachee lost a wider perspective and would benefit from seeing the issue from a variety of observation points. They would, hopefully, end up with a richer picture – perhaps in colour where before they saw monochrome.

It is not assumed that the coachee will leave the session with a clear, determined policy as to what to do next. Instead, they might simply be more in touch with a variety of options previously not thought about or respected. In this instance, leaving with a state of mind of uncertainty and confusion could be a more constructive outcome than exiting with a 'hell for leather' determination to deal with the matter 'once and for all'.

In coaching, as in consultation, it also needs to be recognized that what happens *between* formal sessions is at least as important as what happens in the sessions themselves. This time provides the space to think about matters raised and to see whether ideas considered in the sessions are relevant to everyday life. Do they further their understanding? Perhaps most importantly, do they offer a more constructive way for life and work?

Chapter 34

Mentoring

We also need to consider the practice of mentoring. As I understand it, mentoring is closely related to what used to be called 'role consultancy'. As in coaching, two individuals work together to discuss the role of the mentee. However, there are subtle differences. The relationship is not hierarchical: one does not have authority over the other in organizational terms. If there is an element of authority, it is likely to arise from experience. One would assume that the mentor has a greater degree of organizational experience than the mentee, although not necessarily of the mentee's specific role.

The task is to foster a 'learning from experience' approach in the mentee, based on their work and institutional role. Mentoring has aims of empowerment and confidence building, and works towards a thoughtful and modest managing of one's role.

Mentoring needs to be differentiated from supervision. In supervision, the supervisor is supposed to know better than the supervisee how to conduct oneself professionally, and is, therefore, licensed, and required, to make suggestions. In many cases, it is also a component of the supervisor/supervisee relationship that the supervisor has the power to influence, if not decide, whether the supervisee can qualify for whatever position or qualification they are embarked on.

This power relationship between the two influences the learning process. This influence can either be in the direction of helping and fine-tuning the talents of the supervisee or can take the form of stifling the talent and creativity of the student, thus forcing them into institutional compliance that might be detrimental to all concerned.

What all of the above-mentioned processes and interventions have in common is the tussle between compliance and creativity. A certain degree of personal compliance and an agreed way of conducting business, is essential in any organization. However, it also needs to be recognized that, with time, processes become bureaucratized and lose their original meaning. A form of institutionalization, even ossification, thus sets in. This pattern is sometimes beautifully revealed by children asking questions, 'Why, why, why?' Initially parents will answer the questions as best they can but eventually they snap with, 'Because I say so!'

The message in institutions is often equally one of 'Because I say so', i.e. 'that's the way we do things here'. There is, of course, a marvellously reassuring element of consistency, security, and clarity to this sort of response, but at the same time, it can highlight the 'out of touch' element of the organization in relation to the ever-changing environment.

In order for the institution to survive, there, therefore, has to be an awareness of the outside world, and this is often brought in with the emotional and professional 'luggage' of new appointees. New ideas are then met face-to-face with the in-house requirement of compliance put forward by the organization and its institutional members. It is this creation – dealing with the crosscurrents of conservatism and innovation – that is so necessary for the ongoing health of the organization.

Consultancy, coaching, mentoring, and supervision all provide different fora and settings for the work of intercourse and interchange between existing and future ways of functioning.

Chapter 35

360-degree feedback

360-degree feedback, in a variety of forms, is an increasingly used tool for assessing individuals and their functioning. For a start, it is a marvellous opportunity to study an individual's defence mechanisms: 'they don't know me!', 'it's a cultural issue', 'that feedback is based on envy!', 'nothing new that I haven't heard before', etc. At the heart of coaching and feedback, lies the tenet 'do no harm'. What does that mean? Giving feedback about an individual's strengths does no harm, apart from possibly feeding hubris and omnipotence in the subject concerned. But giving feedback about problematic areas can feel as if it is doing 'harm', at least from the perspective of the recipient. If they are to learn from the experience, they will need to dismantle some aspects of their behaviour and splice in others. They might further see this activity as harmful.

Therefore, one could ask: is a '5' rating for the coach a sign of competence and sensitivity, or is it a case of mutual idealization? For example, 'I love your input, and you love me (and the dean or president will love me and keep on hiring me!)'. The individual concerned will rest in comfort, assured that there is no need to change their behaviour.

Chapter 36

Counselling, therapy, and psychoanalysis

No discussion of intervention would be complete without some discussion of the triad of counselling, therapy, or even psychoanalysis. They all share the assumption that the inner world dynamics of individuals have an effect on their personal lives. In the context of this book, the assumption is that inner world phenomena may have a detrimental effect on the individual him or herself, and/or on their relationship with colleagues, clients, and the greater workforce. I suggest a 'negative' influence because if the inner world dynamic were seen as constructive, no one would consider any one of the above professions as having relevance, at least as legitimate interventions supported or paid for by the individual and at times by the organization.

There may, therefore, be a 'coach or couch' dilemma to be considered. It would be unusual for a coaching session not to, at some point or other, come across elements of the personal life of the individual; it may indeed function as an entry point into the no-man's-land between work and home life. Both parties must acknowledge entrance into this and any work done within it should be interpreted in relation to the coachee's work role. For example, if the issue arises of tense and rivalrous relations between members of their work team, it would be legitimate to enquire whether this was a new experience for the coachee or whether she or he had experienced it before in previous work or personal settings.

If the latter is true, it may put the present-day issue into a different perspective. Rather than only being a specific 'here and now' problem of the current work group, it could be partly down to the way in which the coachee relates to others in general. The present occurrence may be a manifestation of a life-long pattern.

If it becomes clear that it is likely to be an aspect of the coachee's method of relating, the question then arises 'what is to be done'. In all likelihood, it would not be appropriate for the coach to venture further into past patterns of the individual's life. The coach may instead remind the individual that there are more personal, clinically based, interventions available. The topic of counselling and psychotherapy can then be discussed, but the decision to embark on a clinical journey should ultimately be left to the coachee.

It is, in my view, counterproductive for the HR department of an organization to advise a so-called 'problematic employee' to have therapy. Such a move is generally perceived as judgemental and negative. It hardly ever leads to the individual concerned taking up the 'offer' and often exacerbates the problem. In institutional terms, it is also inclined to further push the individual into a scapegoat role – the associated problems of which discussed are at length above.

It must be understood that counselling, therapy, or in-depth analysis may be an extremely helpful process for the individual and the way they lead their life, both personally and in work. However, the portal of entry into these processes should be via personal decision, rather than through workplace induced pressure.

Chapter 37

Awaydays

Apart from the above-mentioned interventions, there are other institutional events that I shall briefly examine. At the forefront of these is the so-called 'awayday'. This activity can take many shapes. Some are very helpful, others a waste of time and, in fact, destructive.

Presumably, the term originally meant getting away – physically, structurally, and emotionally – from one's routine work setting.

This has the advantage of enabling individuals to adopt a somewhat different state of mind in relation to their work, their colleagues, and their organization.

If, however, the awayday takes place in the same setting, both structurally and emotionally, as that of one's everyday work, then the chances of being able to adopt a different perspective are substantially diminished. If, on top of that, the managing, leading, or chairing of the day runs along the same lines as one's everyday work–life, then the chances of creating an effective 'awayday' state of mind are even further reduced. Such an event might more appropriately be called a 'general staff meeting'.

For an awayday to have a sufficiently creative element, not only the setting but also the management should be different. Preferably, an independent outsider would chair the meeting or at least consult to it. It is also useful to remember that what happens in between sessions – the informal meetings and conversations – are often at least as effective in pursuing the task as the formal ones. Having an arrangement that includes a night away from home may also result in a more relaxed state of mind and, therefore, ease creative contribution to the overall task.

An effective awayday has sufficient clarity about what the task, topic, or expectation is, but also a structure that allows for innovation of thinking. It is also important for a method of harnessing the beginning, middle, and ending states of mind to be included in the design of the day. Leaving the event should leave participants with some idea of what has been achieved and what is to be achieved in future, by whom, and by when. Having had a good time is, no doubt, beneficial for all concerned, but is not sufficient to be a worthwhile primary task of the awayday.

Other events are also used for staff or organizational developments. These include outward bound events, topic-specific conferences, and group relations events, among others. Some are for formal educational purposes, others, such as the group relations conferences, are temporary learning institutions which give members the opportunity to learn from their own in-conference experience about such matters as authority, leadership and followership, delegation, and group – and inter-group – dynamics of various sizes. In these conferences, external staff need to be available to foster and facilitate the individual members' learning processes.

Chapter 38

Open space events

The largest forum available for organizational development, at the time of writing, is the so-called 'open space event'. This, in essence, provides a venue capable of accommodating the entire membership of the organization or organizations concerned. It provides a structure of separate spaces and timetables, and an overall topic, for example, a proposal to amalgamate three separate institutions into one large one. Individuals are given a platform to propose ideas of relevance to the task, to recruit members to work with them on the topic, and to come up with proposals which are then made public on the open space noticeboard. Members are free to come and go, to be committed to one or other group, idea or cause, or to be institutional 'tourists'.

It is key with all of these events that thought is given to how learning achieved during the programme is to be applied afterwards – in the life and work of the individual participants and their organizations.

Chapter 39

In-house staff support systems

These take a variety of forms. The worst form, in my view, is captured by the phrase, 'my door is always open'. This is meant to show that the person concerned is always available for, and open to, contact with members of the organization. It may be so, but this, in itself, raises the question of what sort of management and/or leadership can be achieved when the individual is constantly available for interruption. Furthermore, while the statement implies immediate and receptive contact, it does not take into account that in front of many a so-called open door sits a watchdog in the form of the personal assistant who is anything but accommodating. While sounding open and friendly, it can actually have the opposite effect.

One could interpret this dynamic as: 'I cannot bother to set aside a regular time to meet with you, but if you can find your way through the obstacle course we might meet'. This process of contact is not conducive to good communication.

Having a specific time set aside on a regular basis to meet with staff in relation to their work roles is essential. If this is respected by both sides, it opens successful channels of communication. But here, too, there are pitfalls. Constant interruption, taking telephone calls, looking at the computer screen rather than the individual concerned, reading and sending texts, all give a clear message: 'I cannot really be bothered to give you my full attention'. Behaving in this manner encourages others to do the same: 'if the boss can behave in this way, then it must also be acceptable for me'. This creates a climate of pseudo-attention and pseudo-communication that is likely to 'infect' the entire organization. What is not a good model for family and couple communication is certainly not a good model in institutional practice.

In many organizations there is also the fear that speaking your mind about problems in the workplace might be held against you, putting at risk your employment or position in the pecking order. The advice often given is not to be open about the issues lest there be litigation. Not being open can, of course, lead to the belief that the problem one has is unique. It also means that colleagues and others in the organization cannot learn from the situation and address the institutional issues.

The recent development and adoption of Schwartz Rounds, particularly in hospitals, goes some way to remedy the problem. All members can attend the presentation and discussion brought by staff members who air their experience of problems, the result being a welcome openness and the possibility of addressing the problematic issues raised.

Emails are a further problem. Ostensibly, they are there to foster and improve communication. In reality, they can reduce personal contact and communication, and provide an endless distraction from the important difficulty of conducting oneself in the role. Looking at, and possibly responding to, 250 emails a day is not necessarily work; it can function as a flight *from* work. At the same time, it masquerades not only as work, but as hard and important work. In particular, the process of copying others into email correspondence, while presented as the distribution of information, is, in effect, the dilution of personal role-related responsibility.

To streamline the email process, it is essential to incorporate a filter, or a system of filters, to remove all irrelevant messages from one's primary inbox. Trust and delegation can play an important role in ensuring only key messages get through. When the 'filter' is an employee – often the deputy or personal assistant – they must be fully empowered to act effectively. If they do not have all the necessary information, for example, calendar access, the system will inevitably lead to confusion, double booking, upset, and grievance.

Similarly, thought needs to be given to the process of delegating authority to someone else to act on your behalf during annual or personal leave. Although a backlog of work will occur if this is not done, it may be more important to take the opportunity to see how the organization functions in your absence. You may discover how and whether your deputy did or did not manage the task of acting in lieu; who slacked or behaved negatively in your absence; and what person unexpectedly shone and needs further encouragement.

From a personal point of view, returning to work after an absence also gives one opportunities, temporarily, to adopt an outsider state of mind, at least in part. Observing the organization, and the organization's effect on one, can lead to beneficial insights and interventions. The absence and return should, therefore, be taken as a learning experience for all involved.

The outside observer state of mind can, however, lead to a degree of unfamiliarity and discomfort that is hard to bear, both in the self and others.

Equally, the organization having awaited the return of the absent member would by far, at an unconscious level, prefer to assume a 'business as usual' state of mind, than having to negotiate the uncomfortable state of a familiar figure returning with an unfamiliar state of mind and all the feared potential turmoil that it might entail. This is of particular relevance when the individual concerned has returned from, say, a management or leadership course with a reputation for having an effect on its participants.

While lip service is paid to the welcoming of new ideas, at an unconscious level the last thing on earth that both the remaining members and the organization itself want is change and potential disruption.

The traditional institutional defence is thus to swamp the returning member with a multitude of tasks and decisions accumulated in his or her absence that ensures that there is absolutely no time or space for a thoughtful re-entry and the possibility of finding applications for one's learning. Instead, one is immediately forced back onto the well-known tramlines of previous behaviour. The 'danger' of change thus soon passes, and the remnants of the learning experience take the form of the occasional business school T-shirt, a global network that is essentially social, and feedback to the other organizational members along the lines of, 'it's a wonderful experience, you must go and see for yourself'.

In the meantime, the returning individual is relieved of the task of having to apply new thinking and practice. He or she can instead get on with being busy, dealing with everything that has accumulated. It, therefore, takes very little for both individual and organization to revert to their original pattern of functioning.

I am here, perhaps in a cynical way, sketching the worst possible outcome of such interventions. But I do so in the hope that in spelling out the potential risks on the path ahead, the pitfalls may be avoided.

Chapter 40

Other support structures

Particularly in the public sector and in the voluntary sector – 'people' industries – it is common to have regular, scheduled staff meetings. The supposed task of these meetings is to vent any stress and emotions arising from the work, and in doing so to improve the capacity of the staff to continue in their roles. In a well-run structured meeting all comments are related to the task of the organization.

Example

The staff group of an adolescent unit: an elderly conservative male stands for an authoritative, possibly authoritarian, response to the misdeeds of an adolescent patient. The argument he has with a forgiving, relaxed, young female member of staff should not be interpreted as an interpersonal personality clash between the two. It is, in fact, the two members of staff verbalizing and debating the appropriate mix of authority and forgiveness that is needed when proceeding through the rocks and whirlpools of the adolescent process.

Often, however, staff debate is left unlinked to the primary task of the organization. Its unconscious processes, and in such instances of 'letting fly' one's emotions or feelings about other members of staff, only adds to the inevitable difficulties of performing one's work role and is likely to create additional interpersonal difficulties.

In attending and conducting staff meetings such as the one described above, it is essential to keep in mind the underlying processes endemic in the organization. It also needs to be understood that, apart from the psychological processes that occur in the unconscious of *all* organizations, there are specific unconscious issues that occur in specialist organizations. These need to be taken account of when working in, managing, and leading such organizations.

Example

As mentioned previously, the constant underlying anxiety in the petrochemical and nuclear industries is of catastrophic accidents. All emphasis is thus on safety and prevention. Hand in hand with this goes denial and carelessness.

Example

A care home is 'exposed' as being a place of neglect and abuse of the elderly inhabitants. Staff behaviour is described as 'deplorable' and prosecutions are initiated. However, it should be understood that the emotional impact of day on day work with demented, disabled, incontinent individuals is extremely draining. The staff at times flip into angry, callous, and retaliatory behaviour. Any organization working in this field needs to make provision for adequate and constant staff support to minimize the risks of staff and patient abuse. Keeping an eye open for symbolism is also a very worthwhile activity.

Example

During an awayday event there was a complaint that some of the chairs were too high for some of the people in the meeting to sit comfortably and to have their feet on the ground. No doubt, any short person would have sympathy for this sort of concrete problem. On the other hand, it might also be seen as a beautiful metaphor for people feeling uncomfortable about the meeting, feeling 'too short' to participate fully. It certainly is the concrete former, but could also be a manifestation of the symbolic latter. An interpretation of the symbolism would be inappropriate, whereas getting some lower chairs would help. In addition to new chairs, it is helpful to consider that some people might feel side-lined, and that efforts made in the management of the meeting to ensure their inclusion would be most valuable.

Example

A man comes to a consultation, and the first thing he says is 'my battery is quite flat – have you got somewhere where I can plug it in?' It is obvious that he is talking about his mobile phone or laptop, but is he also symbolically talking about his state of mind? His morale? It is worth considering.

Conclusion

The essence of this book is the notion that, in order to manage one's personal and organizational life, one needs to have an understanding of the processes that manifest themselves in all areas of one's life. The key is the realization that one's picture of the world and its functioning is solely one's own. It is not the way anybody else sees it. This sobering reality means one has, on a daily basis, to monitor not only one's own assumptions but also make allowance for the fact that any work or social intercourse requires an acknowledgement of other perspectives. It requires us to respect each other's rights to have views other than ours, and the need to work with others at reaching some sort of ongoing accommodation within our professional relationships. Von Clausewitz, the Prussian military thinker, said 'war is the continuation of diplomacy'. What this book has been attempting to create is a 'good enough' climate of understanding to enable ongoing thoughtfulness and communication and thus, if possible, to avoid a war-like state of mind.